Soundless Impressions

Poems

DAVID JAFFIN

First published in the United Kingdom in 2016 by
Shearsman Books
50 Westons Hill Drive
Emersons Green
Bristol BS16 7DF

Shearsman Books Ltd Registered Office
30–31 St. James Place, Mangotsfield, Bristol BS16 9JB
(this address not for correspondence)

www.shearsman.com

ISBN 978-1-84861-400-0

Distributed for Shearsman Books in the U. S. A.
by Small Press Distribution, 1341 Seventh Avenue, Berkeley, CA 94710
E-Mail orders@spdbooks.org
www.spdbooks.org

Production, composition, & cover design: Edition Wortschatz, a service of
Neufeld Verlag, Schwarzenfeld/Germany
E-Mail info@edition-wortschatz.de, www.edition-wortschatz.de

Title picture:
Qi Baishi (Qi Huang, 1864–1957),
"Little magnolia branch" ("Kleiner Magnolienzweig"), ca. 1934,
China ink and light colour on paper, 46 x 29 cm
Photography: © bpk-Bildagentur / Museum für Asiatische Kunst,
Staatliche Museen zu Berlin / Jürgen Liepe

Printed in Germany

Contents

With continuing thanks to
Marina Moisel
for the preparation of
this manuscript

For me good poetry has always meant a unity between sound, sense, image and idea – a prevading mood-tonality. There must never be a word too many – poetry as the art of compression, "saying the most by using the least". The main adversary is cliché – using words the way they've been usually used. Poetry should take-on a cleansing function, letting words and the context-of-words shine again as newly-minted coins. Every poet tends to have his own clichés, his own oft half-routine ways of expression. These must be discovered and eliminated. Such "contaminated" poems are those ca. a quarter-of-the-whole which will be discarded.

My poetry actually "began" through a reading Wallace Stevens gave at the YMHA in New York in the early 1950s – the best of these poems such as *13 Ways of Looking at a Blackbird, The Idea of Order at Key West, 2 Letters* (in *Poems Posthumous*), *Peter Quince at the Clavier, The Snowman* … were republished in the excellent obituary on Stevens which appeared in *Time Magazine*. I sent Stevens some of my earliest poems and he responded with words I'll never forget: "You must be your own hardest critic." I've always taken those words to heart. Aside from these particular poems of Stevens the central influence on my poetry has continued to remain those great adagios of Joseph Haydn, where space, measure, and sound derive a lasting unity-of-sense.

My earliest books are generally of a quality which continues to satisfy my own aesthetic sense, they were very deliminated in theme. After years of devoting myself to another calling, that of preaching and writing about Jesus the Jew (via the Old Testament) in post-Auschwitz Germany, poetry suddenly and unexpectedly overcame me on a train to Dortmund in 1989. Ever since then, and especially in the 21st century, I've become perhaps the most prolific of poets, and that in my aging years. Why?

Because of the many-interior-tensions within my very-being and also because of my depth of interest and education in various fields. Those tensions, so explicit in my poetry are between The Christian and The Jew, between being an American and a German, between an active and an interior religious life, between time and timelessness … I am a very one-sided person, but those fields I've made my-own I've depthed as well as I could: literature, classical music, art, faith and religion, the nature of history, human understanding, love, nature, animal-life, aging and death …

The poetic process is for me at least two fold: either words come over me and demand a word discovery of their true sense; or ideas on this or that linger in my mind until they can find poetic expression. This is the more difficult for me. The ambiguity of language, open endings, levelled meanings seemingly "contradictory" sense of meaning are characteristic of my intuitively conceived poetry. Each poem should be read at least two or three times, and once, at least, aloud, to discover their intrinsic musicality.

I want to thank my dear wife of 52 years, Rosemarie, my muse, for that love, which is at the essence of my very being.

David Jaffin

P. S. I've often been asked why I break words between lines. As Lenore, one of my most perceptive readers said, "You don't really break words between the lines, but place them within the entire rhythmic flow of the poem."

As my poems are extremely condensed I don't want words, especially the longer ones, to be "hanging out", therefore this very musical need for such a continuing on. Word-break, if one wants to call it that, means that these words must be put back together again, almost as if they've become recreated, newly realized.

If only time

that restless
inquisitor

of a taste
ful momentary

ease could stand
erect permanent

ly-so!

One can't

really love-e
nough a Christ

tied-and-bound
to one's own

imprison
ed-self.

R. H.

always there
when needed

mostly quiet
ly reassur

ing almost
self-effacing

ly present.

Crocodile

s watering that
place hungry

for flesh the
gazelles

graceful
ly though in

stinctive
ly holding-

close to their
life-breath

ing source.

These "newly-

acquired dis
covery word

s" angle a
poem to its

sufficient
ly pre-deter

mining end.

Parasail

floating-on-
air as light

as the wind
s could carry

that moment
ary ease of

self-sustain
ing impress

ions.

Art Questions (12)

a) Why has pain

even of the
crucifixion

remained so
foreign to

Stefan Loch
ner's aesthet

ic sensibilit
ies.

b) Why are Raph

ael's Madonna
and Child so

perfectly
self-encompass

ing when Jesus
so-early se

parated Him
self from the

source of His
mother's all-

consuming love.

c) Why are Grüne

wald's master
pieces so punct

uated with
pain's actual

callings when
love's the

ultimate
source of

Christ's very-
being.

d) Has the light-

dark redemption-
duality of

Rembrandt'
s self-port

raits limited
the scope of

his own per
sonal-identi

ty.

e) Hommage à Didi Huberman

Why did it
take art his

torians so
long to real

ize the true
source of Fra

Angelico's
Annunciation'

s so secret
ly-elusive

claims-on-
us.

f) Why have art-

historian
s so long pre

ferred Canaletto'
s architect

onic aesthetic
when Guardi

(as Thomas Mann)
realized the

brooding-lyrical
qualities of

Venice's half-
sunken time

less mysterie
s.

h) If Rembrandt'

s Man with the
Gold Helmet

was not paint
ed by himself

Whom of his con
temporarie

s could have
conceived such

a sovereign
painterly-

greatness.

i) What's the

mysterious
cause of Georges

de la Tour and
Velázquez

having twice-
painted two

of their sup
reme master

pieces.

j) Ode à Ruskin

Is the lyric
ally-refined

aesthetic
of much relig

ious art of
intrinsical

ly lesser qual
ity than con

ceiving man'
s increasing

self-import
ance.

k) Was/why

the Christ-
child of Bell

ini's Madonna
of the Meadow

s really dead-
alive for His

life's true-
callings.

l) Has abstract

art denied
the possibili

ties of a
faith-imbued

transcend
ing express

iveness.

m) Why has

the cultural
ly consummate

classical
Greek art fail

ed to encompass
the higher-

realms of
painting and

music.

Railed-balcon

ies to the
sea as if its

rhythmic-
sounds could

become metall
ically in

tent.

Emotional

ly short-breath
ed persons

more-like
trees branch

ed-tight
from much of

their excess
ive leaf-climb

s.

Shadow

ing birds mo
mentary dark

ness-spell
s.

Cliché

ing oneself'
s the perpet

ually chang
ing behind-

the-scene-dan
gers of inno

vative poetry.

Card Players (3)

a) Georges de

la Tour's game
of cheat and

deceptive
eyes circling

a sense of
their-own ir

retrievable
gain.

b) With Cézanne

the cards as
upright as

the players
themselve

s a static
game of inter

ior-resolve.

c) Passing the

time away

has left so
much (played

or not) indis
tinctly be

hind.

For Rosemarie

Does the smil
ing composure

of your stead
ied face and

eye me in
to those har

boured shore-
realms-of-

ours.

She too-much

younger-felt
for her very-

good as if
age was but

a timeless
pursuit of

continuous
self-denial.

New friend

s as doors o
pening to

close the
spaces of those

left so in
adverting

ly behind.

With thanks

to A. W. Salomone

who relativ
ized me to my

hungried-
need for find

ing something
more-substan

cial.

She couldn'

t smile how
ever-much

tried-it-on
still couldn'

t.

a) He was that-

kind-of-person
who made his

weight felt
as if shadow

s could be
come heavily

ground-based.

b) Too-much be

came never-e
nough-for-

him as that-
kind-of-sym

phony (late
romantic)

so big that
however-much

of tonal-col
or couldn't

possibly keep
its formal-de

mands intact.

Intimacy

They lowered
their voice

s together
when those

fires began
to-dim as an

untouchable
sign of per

soned-intima
cy.

With thanks (3)

a) With thanks (again)

to M. S.

as the poison
ed-snake of

his desert-for
saken-time

s She raised
him to the

gradual green
ness of an o

asised half-per
manency.

b) to W. W.

on that dirt-
road-path of

the one not-
yet-paved

to its rout
ed singular

ity You became
his Staupitz

guiding path-
finder.

c) And most-

finally to
Rosemarie

where love
bloomed from

those earthed-
down silence

s as winter
ed flower

s to a lost-
found constan

cy.

Aging (5)

a) If there'

s a continu
ing unity of

body-soul-spir
it Why these

almost Hades-
like exhaust

ing-spells and
the (yet) re

viving love-
sourced spirit

ual-poetic
realms.

b) when the

past (though

vitally awak
ened) become

s (neverthe
less) as those

sunken-ship'
s treasure-

loads.

c) those constant

ly (though

space-time re
curring fear

s) of a less
er-vacated per

son left all-
at-once to

itself alone.

d) the daily

scaled-image

of Amos' 3rd
vision too-

weighted or
light-found

that uneas
ily balan

cing self.

e) despite de

clining

strength dis
covering one'

s own light-
dark alternat

ing time-rhy
thms.

Not-the-doctor'

s choice a
woman who chose

light-envision
ing blindness

to life-save
her wombed

dark-inhabit
ing daughter.

Those-who-

survive the
fittest for

a life-secur
ing future

but not those
fibered with

the finest of
ethic and moral

integrity.

Low-tide (5)

a) feeds on

the residue

of inescap
able waved-

down rhythmic-
impulse

s.

b) Low-tides

poeming the
silent shore

s of those
word-elusive

intimacie
s.

c) Low tide'

s breath
less moment

s when time
seems settled-

down passive
ly-intent.

d) when walking-

the beach be

comes soundful
ly-aware.

e) when the

sea has calm
ed to its

unspeakable
depth.

Wind-trac

ing those ines
capable sound-

imprint
s.

Was he hid

ing from his
secretly-

lonely self-
indwelling.

Time-sitting

as if the
word-itself

had come to
a stand-still

immovably
there.

a) Street light

s dimly-sensing
the emptied-

depth of our
own interior-

silence
s.

b) Totem-poles

strangely-a
ware of those

unexplored
distance

s of color
ed-imagining

s.

For Corinne and Tom

not a 2nd
choice (as

they first
realized) but

a 2nd-time as
if marriage

had become
its own self-

revealing.

Tom

a poem was
something

you'd always
s known

(those vague
ly shadow

ing moment
s) though

seldom fully-
realised.

Lily P.

the aged
femme-fatale

's last spite
ful words o

pening-up the
festered

wounds from
their closed-

in covering
s triumphant

ly descended
into a piti

less grave.

Pelican

s floating
the celestial

ease of their
ever-expand

ing tidal do
mains.

Dead-ends (6)

a) There must-

be a dead-

end to where
the road stop

s because
there's no

wheres-from-
its-going-

on.

b) The storms

didn't cease
They held-on

the ice and
cold that stopp

ed-time at its
very-source.

c) where man

failed that in

visible source
now steering

its own course
for an unmapp

ed future
less realm.

d) where even

love seemed

cut-off
cold and per

ishable no
longer origin

ed untouchab
ly adrift.

e) Kingdom-of-

that-other-

death the
numbed-future

of a space
less even god

less-void.

f) what happened

to her (as-to-
so-many-other

s) timeless
ly in that un

told woods
where they

found her
bloodied and

nakedly alone.

Two "unforgiveable" sins (2)

a) of judging o

thers into

the command
ing darkness

of an irrecon
cilable guilt.

b) of a self-

pity that

knows only
the tear

s of one'
s own blind

ing alone
ness.

G. B. *(for Tony)*

getting-better
as those fad

ing imperial-
claims to a

more-subdued
if less-sub

stantial
daily-exampl

ed learn-as-
it-goes firm

ness.

N. D.

still an enig
ma addicted-

down to the
lower-level

s raised-up
by his future

wife to support
her with a

strength of
growing-con

viction ran-
all-their-

money-through.

Can thought

s become re
flective

ly-glassed
or do they

distill the
depth of an

increasing
clarity.

Life-worthy

is death-worth
y of life's

all-encompass
ing claims-

on-us.

It's often

the unsaid
(implied)

those between
ed-silence

s revealing
more than e

ven the word-
itself right

ly-express
ing.

Is love

(then) a lapse
of that self-

I its lesser
being an over

coming full
ness.

This oncom

ing-dawn seem
s more like

weightless
thought

s light-en
compassing.

Flat-sand'

s far-out
stretches of

the mind's
levelled-down

time-secur
ing.

Shuffle-

boards even-
swing of num

bering-down
self-enclos

ing time-se
quence

s.

Linda child

less though
childful li

brarian i
magining the

colored-depth
of their first

word-sensing
s.

Prepared (4)

a) Can one be

prepared for
the loss

of what's become
so much a

part of self
that one isn'

t without
it.

b) Can one be

prepared for
a life out

of that womb
ed protect

ive self-en
closing dark

ness.

c) Can one be

prepared for
one's own

time-changing
explicitly

always-other
wise self-be

ing.

d) As there'

s really no
means for e

ver preparing
for life's

always-becom
ing as those

procession
al clouds

wind-involv
ing.

Moments (6)

a) At what mo

ment does life
become its

own ever-e
volving

self.

b) When does a

poet realize
it's all-

been-said.

c) Can time be

held as a multi-
colored self-an

swering butter
fly netted

for that al
ways-now.

d) when a poem

ever-elusive
ly realize

s its own
pre-determin

ing form.

e) when death

realizes its
completely-

own.

f) It may

never-return
that moment

that become
s especial

ly-poemed
still tense

perceptive
ly-near.

The Wind in the Willows (2)

a) that child-

like other-
side to my fa

ther's wishful-
ways of self-

realizing.

b) where Aesop

as British
now as ani

mals become
universal

ly-human.

America (4)

a) a nation

once again di

vided right-
down-the-

middle of
its very-be

ing.

b) The red

and the blue
as the blue

and the grey
separated-

flagged to
blood-sourced

historical
ly-diverse

values.

c) Even the

Great Compro
mise of 1850

left each
side running

for those
still unre

claimed o
pen-space

s.

d) "The-free-

and-the-brave"
can they

brave this e
ver-tighten

ing knot.

These soft

and mild wave
s soothing

ly voiced the
shores recept

ively-intent
composure.

Rebecca's

Grandmother

last-minute
lady exchang

ed bride-groom
and best-man

two weeks be
fore the marr

iage as if
she knew-best

what she didn't
quite know

for a cer
tained before-

hand.

M. P. (5)

a) Don't ever

go-by-appear
ance even pro

fession He
highschool

line-backer
Prison-direct

or always
ready to lend

a helpful hand
touched as

soft as a con
tinual safety-

guarantee.

b) No one

(not even he
himself)

could follow
the guide-line

s of where the
future would

be calling
his certain

(but still ten
tatively)

time-holding
grasp.

c) She one of

the few I've
known to defend

at a moment'
s notice the

right from
wrongly off-

balancing.

d) Stella that

white-soft cur
ly blindness-

of-a-dog e
ven nightly-

sensing read
ily-attuned.

e) Places as

that softly-
enclosed-one

foreigned
with dissemb

ling picture
s yet held to

a closeness
of the hear-

and-word.

Little thing

s that kept
his world in

close-and-
tight as a

child blanket
ed in the

moon's consol
ing nearness

of touched-re
flection.

"Head-over-

heels" but
when securely

landed it took
years to dis

cover a last
ing common-

place of be
neign compos

ure.

Only after

did he real
ize why the

rain had been
voiced in an e

ver-changing
(even varied

coloring)
rhythmic-

phrasing.

Glass-

confines that
kept the sea'

s continuous
callings (if

only momentar
ily) closed-

off.

As a child

trying to
catch the color

ed falling-of-
leaves as if

the rhythmic-
pulse-of-time-

itself could
be but momen

tarily held
tight-in

close.

Snow over

coming even
those sloping

hills of land
scaping remem

brance.

Those beach

up-holding
colored um

brellas often
spacing noth

ing-more than
shadowing

perspective
s.

He didn't

realize he'
d been contin

ually retrac
ing his own

steps until
those foot-

prints faded-
out as his

facial image
as well.

She'd al

ways walked be
hind her hus

band's unalter
ing-step

until he
died and her

own shadow
s couldn't

keep pace
anymore.

Why if the

bible forbid
s "star-gazers"

(Isaiah) did
they find their

cosmically-
routed way

rightly-tim
ed to Bethle

hem the true
source of

light-itself.

Sensed-down

turtles encom
passing the

cool water
s of insatia

ble rest.

The great

Blue Heron
proud and stat

uesque confirm
ing an inde

finable length
of motion

less-poise.

a) Has persecut

ion become a
godly means

of perpetual
ly renewing

the lasting bond
s of His e

ternally-true
two-covenant

s.

b) The church

triumphant
ly-flagged

to a finality
of its bottom

ed-down fail
ing cause.

It rained

the night
through those

ever-greened
Floridian

brightness
es.

The most power

ful of popes
and his contem

porary St. Fran
cis tensioned

the church to
an unfathom

ed course of
polarizing-

renewal.

Those speech

less idols of
the Old Testament

resurrected a
new in the end-

time temptation
s of our self-

proclaiming
mastery over

life and even
over the con

summate realm
of death.

When the tro

pical rains
ceased our fine

ly-meshed screen
ed-in-balcony

netted with the
fragile touch-

of-rain-linger
ing soundless-

appeals.

At the war'

s end he re
turned to a

wife who'd
left him for

another and a
house they'

d bare-handed
to its now

self-abandon
ing claim

s.

Identical

twins in-love-
with the same

woman married
to the same

profession
suited (at

considerable
distance

s) to the same
clothes but

the elder-
one died first

not even identi
cally death-

sourced.

Mangrove

forest myster
iously risen

from a sea
seeded to a

depth of per
petual growth.

Sunset-cruise

Was it the
mild-intent

of the wave
s themselve

s or the lyri
cal phrasing

of dolphin
s that moved

our small craft
even beyond

its own self-
confining

scope.

Caloosa (5)

a) an Indian-folk

once touched

with a less-
permanent-

sense of daily-
concerns now

lost in the
fathomed-wood

ed-myth of
these time-for

saken day
s.

b) The Spaniard

s questioned
the human-stat

ure of those
natively re

mote clans
But we should

rather quest
ion the oft in

humane self-as
surance of

their (and
our) wealth-con

suming lust
s.

c) It's the

poetry of that
singular-momen

tary as those
tiny (but rare

ly seen) tree-
climbing crab

s that inhabit
the oft dormant

regions of our
own so exclus

ively person
ed-being.

d) When myth and

dream inhabit
s real-imagin

ary worlds of e
lusive poetic-

coloring
s.

e) For Warren

to celebrate
the living-

death of a
failed cause

of Lee Stone
wall Jackson

Calhoun because
it's soiled

in the blood
of your-own

When the ro
mance-of-his

tory dies so
will the ro

mance-of-love.

Cloud

s slowly mov

ing-in time
fully conceal

ing the wind'
s invisible

message.

He only

fully realized
light through

the total depth
of an all-en

compassing
darkness.

Every creat

ure (even the
lowliest)

realizes an
antenna of its

own so delica
te and refined

that not even
thought or

speech could
possibly touch-

sense its very
intricacie

s.

It's those

increasing
ly spaced-si

lences of the
vastly unheard

far-out aband
oning street

s.

Poeming the

untelling depth
of and imagin

ary coloring
fish at the

very-length of
its poetical

ly-lined hold
ing-tight.

Those deathly

realms-of-deaf
ness when word

s have lost
their time-im

pressing dis
tinction and

meanings blurr
ed-out from

touch he came
to feel that

faces he'd known-
so-well seem

ed as if al
most haunted

with a ghost
ly isolation.

Low tide'

s soft flow
of finely-e

vened time-re
ceding through-

moment
s.

At sea a

distant boat
horizoned

a finality
of his own

wind-search
ing need

s.

New Mexico (4)

a) New Mexico'

s desert-quiet
of almost un

touchable
soundless per

spective
s.

b) New Mexico

because it's
become the

where of Willa
Cather's and

Georgia O'Keeffe'
s dried-boned

dream's seclus
ively pre-in

habited.

c) The call of

Indian land
s once accent

ed with the
stone-rough

edge of tri
bal war-chant

s.

d) What Stephen

Foster's un
known lonely-

desiring S
wanee River be

came his New
Mexico of cac

tus-flowered
spaceless-

ly coloring ex
panse

s.

As if the

dead continue
to inhabit

their over
coming time-

place appear
ances.

The poem as

a mindfully-
dense self-in

clusive pre-
coloring mos

aic of legend
ary-fabric.

She sported

a masculine-
competitive

husky look
deeply-voic

ed tough-skin
ned.

Mild rain

s caressing
the skin'

s warmth-in
flection

s.

Are unseen

birds voiced-
in those leaf-

enclosing
realms of

greened pre
ception

s.

Restless

unease before
the flight as

if night had
become tense

ly closer.

a) Can one

leave the sea'
s changing-rhy

thmic tide
s behind or

will they con
tinue cease

lessly inde
cipherab

ly echoing.

b) These time-

settling sand
s have left

just scarce
ly fleeting

moments be
hind to their

seldom reali
zing inconclu

sive depth
s.

c) The pier

left him
sounding bet

ween two world
s and a wood

ed surface of
timed-reflect

ions.

She had a-

look-about-
her not yet

down-based as
the after-

flight of
bird's seclu

sive shadow
ing.

Sunglass

es in darken
ing times

can't hide
you from your

self however
evasively

it may have
seemed for o

thers.

On the train (8)

a) as if time-

itself was mov

ing the city'
s concrete

silence
s through

the depth of
its very-be

ing.

b) Snow-pause

s as if spac
ing winter'

s light-with
holding inter

ludes.

c) Only a lone

distant bird
realizing

these tree'
s vacant shad

owings.

d) This late

winter sun
closing behind

clouded-imag
ining

s.

e) Train

tracks-in-
snow an al

most certain
ed-sense of

time-continu
ing.

f) Wooded-enclos

ures those in
timacies of

darkening
self-shadow

ings.

g) These hill

s sloping-down
the smooth

nesses of con
templative

timeless ex
posure

s.

h) The slend

er dance-in
clination

s of poeti
cally-appar

ent birch-
woods.

Is spring

not awaken
ing but held

dormant here
self-encompass

ing.

a) Jacob v. Ruis

dael's Water
fall rocky

landscape
(1660s)

Only the ever-
greens watch-

over a world
of transform

ing-change.

b) Van Goyen's

River Landscape

with Parish
Church (1651)

The silent re
pose of another-

world immersed-
in a daily pre-

consuming bey
ondness.

c) Rubens Portrait
of a Capuchin Monk (1635)

Is that Rubens
himself carved-

out with spirit
ual feature

s his own time-
immersing re

flection
s.

d) Those 2nd rank

"Golden Age"
painters knew

more how-to-
paint than to

signify a per
sonal range

of time-sus
pending intuit

ions.

e) Pre-Ruben

s female-nude
s seemed imper

sonally inhabit
ing a lesser

flesh-entic
ing bodied

bloodful
ness.

On the train (4)

a) More window

s than per

sons isolat
ing a sense

of untime
ly-loneli

ness.

b) These winter

ed woods still
toned-down to

a muted time-
remembran

ce.

c) Unconscious-

clues of our
personally-

sourced expos
ures as that

eye-spanned
reach or color

ed-fabriced
self-chosen

clothes the
innuendoe

s of voiced-
inflection

s or (per
haps even)

those self-
concealing

more than
skin-tight

blemishing
s.

d) His eye

s beaked like
a hawk's

flesh-devour
ing instinct

s.

What could ap

pear more self-

satisfying
than the beau

tified seduct
ive coloring

s of in-bred
poisoned

Floridian
snake

s.

America (2)

a) America

where guns
speak louder-

than-word
s innocent

ly defend
ing blood-rid

den.

b) America'

s post-democrat
ic plutocra

cy where mon
ey-raised

tallying-up
votes in column

s of neatly-
earned dollar

s-and-cent
s.

Are house

s faced witness
ing what re

mains unspok
en or are

they simply
windowed

from interior
meanings of

(as yet) an
indefinab

le cause.

Walls can be

come a shadow
ing of stop-

here or
enclose a pro

tective need
for a privacy

of self-reflect
ion.

Do birds

only relinguish
their bright

ness of color
ing when dark

ness subdue
s them into

self-reclaim
ing submissive-

shadowing
s.

a) Boats may

child our
feel for free-

streaming in
terlude

s but sea-
spaced they

hold-us-fast
to an inclus

ive time-dis
tancing.

b) Cool sheet

s may touch-
us into

those seldom
depths of

sleep's on
coming silen

ces.

c) Spring's first

instinctual
light-source

can rise us
ever further

than our own
horizoned

length of
mind-scope.

d) Raphael

our son
may sing-

himself into
those realm

s of unremem
bered sensibili

ties.

Are the sea

sons more a
mirror of our-

own time-revolv
ing appearan

ces.

a) Are dream

s more the un
touched ech

oings of still
unresolved

question
ings.

b) Does a poem

acquire its-
own distinct

ively-appar
ent voice or

does it be
come by means

of it's al
ways-having-

been-there
before.

c) Fear most-of-

all of myself
of eyes that

could meet them
selves in-the-i

mage of dream
ed-awareness.

d) Will the

past become real
ized again as

a 2nd chance
or a forgott

en remembran
ce so alive

as if spoken
through the

depth of death'
s timeless

ly echoing-
fears.

Jews (4)

a) Haven'

t they killed
and hated e

nough in the
East where

those death-
commando

s bloodied-their-
lines-through of

helplessly
trembling Jew

s.

b) Are we Jews

(Israelis) call
ed again to

pay-the-price
in the image

of a distant
ly unknown

Christ for the
thirsting sin

s of our a
vidly-intent a

venger
s.

c) They only be

came totally-
Jewed in the

bloodied unan
swering claim

s of Christ's e
ternal redempt

ion.

d) Berlin u

glied-desecrat
ed city of

those glove-
surgeoned

death-decree
s Jewed-again

as if out of
that “final

solution” re
surrected

in-the-image
of a barely-

sensed spring-
timed revival.

His secret-e

nemy sworn with
in the depth

s of his-own
brooding a

vengence
s.

The prophet

ic word speak
s “louder

than the
sword’s” clean

sing-bright
ness blood-a

vowed.

A room of

glassed and
closed-in

book-cases
untouched

from use title
s time-fad

ed heir-loom
ing a lost

and never
found again

life-of-their
own.

b) Whatever

those number
s meant hard

ly decipher
able now

stoned (per
haps) as a

form of mea
sured distant-

lengths bet
ween what

and where in a
world of lost

remembran
ces.

c) Our family be

gan in America
our grandpar

ents witness
ing a new era

a new life in
a land unblem

ished from a
ghettoed past

that remained
for us so re

mote that we
lost what we'

d never known
persons place

s in the mist
of a vanish

ing past.

d) Brigadoon

a mythical
highland-

world awaken
ed every hund

red years out
of a timeless

sleep as if
each day had

become a cen
tury of its-

own personed-
anew in a

land with an
unrecorded-

past.

e) Can we read

our friends
back through a

past that's
written-them-

down even bey
ond their own

sense-of-be
ing.

f) Heir

My father

dreamed a
world that'

s (perhaps
s) more-the-

one I'm liv
ing-in-now

But could he re
cognize its

so distant
ly-escaping

place and a
son that left

his unreveal
ed-self be

hind.

Critics

(as therapist
s) often too

self-involv
ed to realize

what they're
so actually-

mirroring'
s even more

of their-own
unresolving-

personed- view.

For Rosemarie

Only love'
s the contin

ual source
of its un

known origin
s.

The flounder

dwells comfort
ably at-the-

bottom of a
bottomless

sea contemplat
ing a world

of soundless
inertia.

a) Perhaps the

butterflie'
s straight-

lined fantasie
s leaf-it to

a momentary
eased-route.

b) Bees honey

ed with too-
much sweet

ness buzz
their daily-

ways irretriev
ably sense-

intent.

c) Why does a

tiger space
its avidly a

lert eyes in-
to-the-dark

of untold
flesh-wounded

design
s.

d) Does the Zebra

hoofed-in
ground-dust

ed allusion
s realize its

inherently
safety-balan

cing geometri
cal-stripe

s.

e) Cats

moon-lit se
creting shad

ows their
hungry-claw

ed instinct
s.

f) Zooed-animal

s on-display
as those theat

rical-person
ages curtain

ed for a hu
man-like presen

tation.

d) Are those

skin-lined in
vasions time'

s way of re
calling its-

own permanent
ly marked-down

feature-show
s.

e) Powder and

cream can't
possibly soft

en the soiled-
erosions

of your daily-
involving es

cape-route
s.

When animal

s ran-out of
their light-

weighted
dream-imagin

ing flight-
source

s.

Classicism

as the Caracci
thought-process

es the even-
mass of pre-

conceived
wholely self-

consistent
draught'

s manship.

Inspiring

You may-have-
sent-them

feet-off
air-balanc

ing sublime-
inhalation

s.

This late

winter sky

cloudful
ly-weighted

as some per
sons I've

known ponder
ously self-en

closing.

Better pre

pared than most
for what can'

t-be-prepared-
at-all Proofed-

at-the-brink
with a pre-find

ing faith
better-prepar

ed (if-that's-
possible-at-

all).

Dvořák op. 51 *(Quartet slow mvt.) (2)*

a) One must have

a soft-heart

for this-kind-
of-music or

one that's
readily taken-

into an irre
vocably sense-

sounding pre
sence.

b) Dumky

quick-beated
dance-rhythm

ic false-
starts into

a fantasied
world of home-

indwelling
heart-certain

ties.

Haydn's sublime op. 76,5 *(slow mvt.) (2)*

a) can-be-play

ed anyway it

wants a pure-
sounding para

disically dark
ly-consuming

beyondness.

b) presto

a never-stop
for-more-than-

a-breath
ed fun piece

of an irre
sistably dia

logued there'
s-always-some

wheres-else.

Beethoven

op. 59,2 Quartet
last mvt. took

the right-route
this time not

power but a
contrapuntal

al whirl-wind
of post-classi

cal ever-punct
uating fineness

es.

Glib'

s the easy
round-about

way from feel
ing-too-

much.

This late

winter's more-
like-a change

able face
(fully) self-

deceiving its-
own pre-concei

ved intention
s.

New house

s here as the
people they

bare witness
to more fit-

for-themselve
s than fit-

in a landscap
ing unison

ed-design.

Was it the

over-coming
fear of Beet

hoven's final
ity or Haydn'

s folk-wayed
initiative

that finally string-
quartet(ed)

its late 19
th century

rebirthed a
waken

ings.

10 Variations on a self-same theme (10)

a) She was like

crossing-a-
bridge that

knew only
her-other-side

left her hang
ing helpless

ly-alone mid-
air.

b) She became so

intent on-the-

sound-of-her
own-voice e

choing-back
worldless

ly-unanswer
ing.

c) Those wind

ing stairs en
closing a dark

ness repetit
ively-indis

tinct.

d) Some person

s inhabit the
clothes (how

ever-alternate
ly-colored)

of-their-own
instinctive

ly-unmistak
able self.

e) She became

more-like circ
ling-a-pond

(small though
self-enclos

ing) that
failed to re

veal her-own
inescapable-

shadowing
s.

f) She became-

for-us like
a book open

ing-out an in
delible-past

of lost
through-cut

paging
s.

g) Where-from-

here's a no-
turning-back

but only a no
where-of-on

coming's sound
lessly-re

mote.

h) We-knew-her-

less-by-know
ing-her-more

like-a-pond
of a self-

enclosing
shadowless-

depth.

i) Are such

windows time-
telling through-

a-length of
speechless

ly self-inhab
iting.

j) Something o

minously-
present at-

an-untelling-
height of a

self-impend
ing there

ness.

With each

friend gone
How much of

our very-per
son become

s lessen
ed to but a

shadowless-
self.

He couldn'

t even trace-
the-flight

of where
that bird left

its so distant
colors horizon

ed-behind.

Is this so

personally
late-winter

ed-moon
closed from

remembran
ce-view still

intently watch
ing through

its steadily
alive-sake.

Are these

fields-of-my-
youth

closing now
as paged-

thought
s timeless

ly viewed.

Time sense (3)

a) When we sat

at those Sun
day-night au

tumnal fire
s and the

remember
ed darkness

seemed (then)
as if scarce

ly flamed-a
live.

b) Can the

softly-muted
designs on

that ceramic
ally-surfac

ing bowl re
round your

hands to
their evasive

ly indwell
ing time-sense.

c) Can what

remains only
imperfect

ly-untouch
ed be recall

ed to its
lifeful

time-impend
ing presence.

If there'

s a-no-way
s-back why

rehearse
its oncom

ing future.

For George

You can't

hold-him-back
because he'

s always a
head-of-him

self carriag
ed to a horse

less water
ing-spell.

For George (again)

"What's normal"
's most-alway

s that ever-
unchange

able scarce
ly definable

run-away-
self.

The poem re

leased not-a-
chance-to-

breathe as if
those breath

less-moment
s had become

timeless
ly-inert.

Some music

can continue
to haunt-one

as a house
that's out-

lived its
only-person

ed-self.

a) This dark'

s become voic
ed with the in

creasing
space of an

impending
stillness.

b) She lay

in a self-en
compassing

bed of pain
ed-silence

s.

c) He'd been

outgrown from
a world so-

changed that
he feared be

ing left-a
lone to its

untouched as
surance

s.

d) This moon

darkly-felt
secretly self-

concealing
its still un

known presen
ce.

e) If there'

s no dialogue
left only

this timeless
pause between

an irrecon
cilable night.

A lone cat (3)

a) A lone cat

chasing the
shadowing

s of its
pawed-enclos

ures.

b) A lone cat

alley-wayed
its seldom

voiceless
ly unformed

smile.

c) Why has the

moon lit this
abandoned

street-cat
to such awak

ening fantas
ies.

Around that

newly-discov
ered corner

he met the
lone heart-

beat of his
still insuffi

cient-self.

Sun ris

ing the close
ly-intent dark

nesses from
his own pre-

meditative
person.

For Rosemarie (3)

a) There should

become an al

ways-increas
ing-gladness

from our daily
self-enclos

ing-together
ness.

b) How subtle

ly bright

you've be
come this mor

ning's pre-
touched flower

ings.

c) The soothing

touch-flow

of your light
ly-inviting

hair with
draws most of

these time-im
pending fear

s.

As a Polonius

I wanted to
tell him

"face-up-to
your-own-in

terior-self"
But he contin

ued to head-
out from such

(perhaps) un
told darken

ing silence
s.

Pavel Haas Quartet 3 (1938)

How can a
work become so

inwardly uni
fied in its so

divisively-
contrary ex

pressive Jewish
ishness.

a) Tulips

self-enclosed
an indwell

ing darkness
of colored-

expanse
s.

b) Bluebell'

s choirs of
child-like

innocent a
wakening

s.

Beethoven's 7th (4)

a) Did that

splendid A
Major key him

into a con
suming dance-

like express
iveness.

b) Allegretto

procession
ally solemn

ly advancing
beyond the

solitary
realms of these

held-down
earthly-enclos

ures.

c) The presto

rhythmical
ly-densed

its repetit
ively (once

fully convinc
ing) declamat

ions.

d) The finale'

s overdone
faust-down re

petition
s echoed (for

me at least)
times once

dangerous
ly soul-

near.

Chopin's E Minor Piano Concerto

feasted Kit
Armstrong'

s nimble fin
gers to take-

offs of their
exclusive

ly sound-
fit presence.

Chopin'

s moon-lit
kind-of-poet

ried me in
to a sunken-

past irretrie
vibly-sensi

tized.

Kit Armstrong'

s Bach encor
ed me back-to-

a-world of
ground-based

depthed-inclus
ions.

Float

ing flower
s watering

the untouch
ed-depth

s of color
ed-design

s.

A naked

tree with a
single large

ly unspoken
bird holding-

tight to
its seem

ingly time
less-intent.

After Theodore Fontane'

s recurring
fears at the

water's uneasy
surfacing

a withhold
ing smooth

ness spread
ing-out time'

s reassur
ing quietude

s.

Aging may be

come a reflect
ive low-tide-

time of wait
ing for what'

s still appar
ently indis

tinctly un
known.

Homilius'

motets oft
more an awak

ening call-to-
voice of an

instinctual
(though alway

s impulsing)
together

ness.

High tide

s soak-out
those fantas

ied sand-cas
tles endeavor

ing-young-child
ren once so

furtively-
aspiring

eye-sen
sed.

Woman with Fan *(Seehaus 1914)*

Seeming
ly poised on

a precipice
of light

ly-endowed
self-suffic

iency.

Lithely-

naked branch
es dance-

like those
still self-es

caping inti
macie

s.

The lowly

worm indulgent
ly rain-soak

ed its self-
expanding

initiative
s.

Doesn't

If he doesn'
t word-you-

right he does
n't (either)

know-you-sen
sed.

Aside

s brief inter
lude's light

ly-sensed
transpar

encie
s.

When person

s become in
distinguish

ably shadow
ed.

He was like

a puppet
pulled-by-

strings
feet left

mostly high-
rised.

This early

spring morn
ing gradual

ly awaken
ed from its

self-shadow
ing night

ly withdraw
als.

Pre-meditat

ed poems sent
enced to that

last degree
of self-den

ial.

For Rosemarie

Beauty re
mains its own

untold mean
s of self-

discovery
as a rose'

s depthed in
folding

s.

As a flow

er's disfac
ed coloring

s so suspic
ion's dead

ly inbreed
ings.

Modern

ism's percuss
ively blemish

ed discoloring
s oft pene

trate a less
er indepth

ed self-guar
antee.

(the process)

as a poem
continue

s to reflect
its refining

unaware still
muted self-

transform
ings.

Some critic

s have learn
ed too-much

to be poem
ed-alive to

what's so re
freshing

ly other
wise.

If each day

could only
take us off-

balancing our
daily pre-con

ceived time-
route

s.

Blue

bells air-
light heaven

ly awaken
ing at the

bottom-down
impending

death-zone
s.

Bartok'

s rhythmic-
urge can still

dance-depth my
slowed down

time-bending
inertia.

Pre-timed

fresh spring
winds frag

rance the
light of a

still unanswer
ing flower-

sense.

When uncertain

ty becames a
shoreless

presence
caught in-the-

midst of these
ever time-shift

ing tide
s.

What's to

believe when
no one know

s "for cer
tain" as if

life could be
come a stop-

watch time
lessly only-

there only-
now.

Israel

Once again
isolated

abandoned
left naked

ly-alone to
the predator'

s meat-hungry
instinct

s.

Birch

woods so grace
fully feminine

standing-out
against some

of the mean
est of cli

mates.

Spring

still so youth
fully unexpos

ed reminds of an
indecisive

maiden's one
day this the

next that
if mirroring

the weather'
s furtive

changeabili
ties.

Our friend

s continue
to kaleido

scope our e
ver-changing

intricate
ly self-involv

ing time-se
quence

s.

If life'

s no-wheres-o
ther than no-

stops aside
Why do those

slow movement
s continue

to depth the
interior

s of our
very-being.

Planning

for a future
that can't

be planned-
for Pink irre

solately stood
brightly self-

convincing
his most color

ed outfitt
ings.

From Wuthering Heights (film) (3)

a) when he knif

ed that ani

mal in-to
the blood-

veins of his
owned pained-

suffering.

b) when man be

comes animall

ed-down to
nature's most

elemental
thirsting-

desire
s.

c) She must

have known
he would nak

ed-her-down
to the long

ing depths of
their irresis

tibly intent
ly-consuming-

passion
s.

Beethoven Piano Quintet with Winds op. 16

a Beethoven
unpreten

cious (and
yet) strong

and original
indwelling.

C. Stamitz Wind Quartet op. 8#2

brightly in
toned Keyed

to the claims
of a sound-

apparent
unity.

Mozart Piano Quintet
with Winds K. 452 Larghetto

a lightly fan
tasied world

even beyond
touch of

time's intel
ing reach.

Poems from the Chinese *(for Neil) (5)*

a) Zhao Mengfu
Autumn Colors on

the Qiao and Hua
Mountains (1296)

so finely
death-enchant

ed as if peopl
ed from the

time-spanned
myths of an ir

reconcil
able past.

b) Ma Yuan (Attributed)

Composing poetry on an
early spring morning 13th c.

Does that poem
bridge his

guests to an a
wareness of

nature's dark
ly-rooted

spring-timed
design

s.

c) Zhao Mengjian

3 Friends of Winter
(pine plum bamboo, 1260)

a persisten
cy of winter'

s life-grasp
ing death-

calls.

d) Ma Lin
In Lamplight

awaiting guests
mid 13th c.

a ceremonial
path-way

leading down
to a recreat

ing-enlighten
ment.

e) Wang Meng

Straw-roofed
Houses on Mt. Tai, 14th c.

as if time
were hanging

skied-high
from its own

timeless
ly transpar

ent-self.

Chung

homeless
ly Vietnam

ese a world
deaden

ed from lost
perspect

ives.

Their house

being cleansed
inside-out

from all sus
piciously

dangerous
pre-concern

s.

She led a

shadowed exis
tence enclos

ed in fear
s that darken

ed her every
thought-in

voking moment.

Wuthering Heights

When nature'
s desolating

nakedness
mirroring

man's vast
ly uninhab

ited self-be
ing.

Time conden

sed as a spid
er's web to

its intense
ly fragile

momentary
design

s.

Times in

waiting land
scaped to a

colorless
depth-down

wind-fore
boding.

If there'

s nothing-
more-to-be-

said when
words become

inexpress
ively self-de

signed.

Christmas

attuned to
jingle-bell

s Easter prett
ily bunnie-card

ed No signs of
Christ in these

soil-stained
blemishing

times-of-
ours.

Daily

lands as Syria
Ukraine des

poiled of
their very-worth

bloodied-down
to the vulture'

s naked-cry
for carrion-

flesh.

If butter

flies light-be
holden could

but signify
a moment of

their still
time-color

ing uncertain
ties.

Poems from the Chinese (2)

a) Ma Yuan

early 13th c.

Spring-Time Walk
ing emptied

spaces the
quietude

s beyond his
thought-reach

tree-bending.

b) Huan Gongwang

14th c.

Nine-pearled
heights not

to be person
ed even climb

ed but scarce
ly tree-touch

ed space-
felt.

Prayer (5)

a) when listen

ing to one'
s own-voice

quiets in
to a space

ful beyond
ness.

b) Chinese art

so different
ly shaped-

form
s a passage

way into
one's own

samed-sensi
bilitie

s.

c) I and Thou (Buber)

poetizes
whatever'

s felt-seen
into a

spaceful
interior

oneness.

d) Silence

may voice
more-of-us

by listen
ing into

its shadow
ful expanse.

e) Where love

realms its-
own increas

ing depth
ed-silence

s.

Pagan poetry

earth-down
flesh-blood

ed animall
ed instinct

ively atavist
ic.

This early

spring's mute
d-pastel

sky-like a
wakening

s.

She window

ed a past
eye-length

ed beyond
her fully-

felt sit-
down lone

liness.

For Rosemarie

Please don't
die-me-out

of these so
pleasurable

daily-recurr
ent together

nesses.

Still life

lit in the
intimacie

s of her
barely-sens

ed shadow
ings.

After the Chinese

when the color
ing pattern

s of her
dress-length

an elongat
ing self-ex

pressive
ness.

Mozart's great G minor symphony

as a snow-
driven storm

no-wheres-o
ther than in

cessantly
called-

through.

Haydn's last great symphony

as if pinna
cled at-a-

measured-
height of

consummate-
reconciliat

ion.

Schubert's "Unfinished symphony"

as complete
as a race

started from
its pre-form

ed finish
ing-line.

Light

ly weight
ed words as

transpar
ent as bare

ly-sensed
after-thought

s.

An immovable

war dug-into
the irreconcil

able depth of
their-own i

deological
front-line

s.

One false-

step or even
the uneven

ed-impact of
a mistaken

ly-read-word
can lead world

s far-off in
creasing

ly adrift.

That young

lady's coy
catch-me-if-

you-shadow
ing-please

but a moment
ary inside-

outs.

Caroussel'

s sit-down-
world of

brighten
ed illusion

ary rhythmic-
return

s.

Chinese

horse-encompass
ing emperor

imperial
ly tracing-

down the fleet
ing shadow

s of feared-
sensed rabb

it-ears.

A blind-fold

ed sleep as
if those fear

ed-recurring
dreams could

be closed-
down from

their itiner
ant time-

flow.

Chinese

finely-aesthet
ic painter

ly brush-
strokes

scarcely re
vealing

full-flesh
ed person

ed-being
s.

Daoist

landscape
s heavenly es

caping our
bottomed-down

worldly-suff
erings.

Chinese

finely-sensed
painters re

new a spirit
ual freshness

through the
subtle innuen

does of retrac
ing tradition

al modes of
poetic-appear

ances.

Mis-under

standing's
often too-much-

of-meeting
less (or es

pecially more)
than only

half-way
there.

She dreamt

of an-alive-
speaking-

mouse awoke
to those has

ty steps of
tiny run-a

way fear
s.

That whole

dry-spelled
winter imagin

ing a softly
blanketing

snow that
only drew cos

ily-nearer
in its bed-

timed cool
ly-immers

ing presen
ce.

Oft-balanc

ing surprise

s most often
when we've be

come too self-
attuned pre-

sensed.

a) That glass-

eyed too-much
book-knowledge-

about-her oft
depthed a

lesser appreciat
ion of other

closely-intent
near-time

pleasure-
feel

s.

b) A near-

time step-

down spider
intently with

holding most-
all of its

self-design
ing precept

ions.

What-could-

have-been's
still intense

ly alive to
your vastly-in

tricate
(though scarce

ly) self-re
vealing mind-

route
s.

The intrica

cies of Haydn'

s piano sonata
s keyed to

a mind-touch
ed finger

ing-response.

A two-level

life as a
house downstair

ed for person
ally self-ac

comodating
intimacie

s and an un
fathomed up

stairs strange
ly remote yet

ghosted with
skeletal-re

membrance
s.

So tempting-

near the naked
ly revealing

need for un
dressing

her neck-seduc
ing touch-

flow.

Academic

ally correct
primly book-

stanced
(though) tig

er-clawed
their blood-

letting in
stinctual

urging
s.

An even-keel concert of Mozart's sonatas K. 576, 570, 282 (2)

a) steadily a

float until
that sudden

ly-depthed
K. 330 andante

shored me in
to its time-

enduring wav
ed-stillness

es.

b) K. 282 slow

mvt. imposing
start varied

in-to a less
er-claimed

toned-final
ity.

"Georg" Benda's later symphonies (2)

a) rough-edged

short-spell

amassed stone-
securing

s.

b) slow mvts.

envision
ing a swan-

like world
softly smooth

ed wave-tim
ing.

For Erich

good fellow
helpful

ly unassum
ing when

needed keep
s this uneas

ing pace-of-
mine steadily

intact.

Unfinished business

Can one bring
one's life

in-order
bound-as-a

book tight
ly-secured

a lasting
testament

of unfinish
ed-business.

For Rosemarie

A one-woman'
s God-given-

beauty is
worth all of

these poem
s papered in

stacks of un
collected i

magining
s.

Sun-high

late February
day sealing

its newly
blue-found

enticing bey
ondness.

Why do these

birds return at
spring at a

height beyond
the reach of

their unspok
en thought-

sense.

Is there a

nother side a

nother way of
warmth and

contentment
beyond our own

reach of but
tentative

ly knowing
where.

He fought

daily on both-
sides-of-self

dug-in-deep
er than even

time could
realize a

spring-
thawed awaken

ing.

"And they lived

happily ever
after" as if

love had be
come an end-

in-itself
not a beginn

ing as if
that darken

ing route
wasn't still

shadowing
his every-

way.

An aging

evergreen
shameless

ly sapped-
down to its

ground-level
poised-iner

tia.

When life

caught-up-
on-him left

him routed
to a wood

s of increas
ingly untim

ed darkness
es.

If only

that lithe
squirrel

could home it
self in me

branch-by-
branch unde

terring
flight-find

s.

Weinberg

s from Kishinev
to Warsaw to

Minsk triang
led a death-

route that
sourced a

blood-stain
ed music in

delibly voic
ed.

Rosemarie

without your
inwardly with

holding there-
self I would

have been
as a statue

poised vacant
ly alone.

The glad

ness of spring'
s unearned

recurring
rebirth

ed Christ'
s resurrect

ing mild-
sway.

"It is ful

filled" Christ'
s lasting

testament
even beyond

the earthly
claims of His

innately e
choing word

s.

Weinberg'

s so many solo
works alone

as he bereft
of family/

home of all
but that lone

ly musical in-
tuning.

We circl

ed that pond
early-in-spring

until it be
gan circl

ing us in
to the cool

depths of
its darken

ed-awaken
ings.

Slight

birds scarce
ly shadow

ing the shall
ow route

s of their
flight-inter

lude
s.

A. B.

brought him
self-up to

his best mode
of selective-

appearance
Paragraph

ed to his
strictly-pre

sent legalist
ic-instinct

s.

Once-again

lecturing
his sleep all-

lined-up to a
most attent

ive audience-
acclaim.

If (as Wein

berg felt) his
God always pre

sent or was
it (also) the

angel-of-death
continuous

ly inhabit
ing-him.

Lights-out

the city as
if rediscover

ing the dark
nesses of its

own very-be
ing.

In the shall

ow depth of
this faint

spring light
the bared bran

ches seem as
if thinned-

down to the
lessening

outline
s of winter'

s all-but-ap
parent-hold.

Homilius'

turn-wheel-
way of word-

winding melod
ic expanse.

Dreams (7)

a) A Night of
dreams that
left him in
escapably
afloat with
no-sure-land
to certain an
evened-sense
of time
and place
person.

b) The past
as if trans
formed in
to what had
n't really
happened
only-now.

c) Dante (at
least) had
been guided
into that
dense forest
of timeless
dreams where
as I as if

shadowing
my own elus

ive thought-
sense.

d) Fictive

persons (al
though they'

d once been
"true-to-life")

hadn't been
true to their

oppressive
ly almost

death-instinct
ual silence

s.

e) Awoke to a

world less-
real because

it had be
come too-much-

there "safe-
and-sound"

ly unappar
ent.

f) Is the King

dom of Dream
s as a lost

appearance
so personal

ly ours sens
ed even beyond

the furtive
claims of

death's own
self-inherent

timeless
ness.

g) If "it all

comes back to
us at the end"

may be this
illusive

ly self-appar
ent dreamed-

continui
ty.

Objects

however still
ed real-me-

back to a
world touch

ably (even ap
parently)

self-contain
ing.

Air invisib

ly there still

realms the va
cant distanc

es of this
samed morning-

bird's poised
look-out

haunt
s.

Self-echoings

It's those
unanswer

ed-letter
s that want

to answer-
me-back if

only as self-
echoing

s.

Our doctor

always out-of-
breath landed

wings-down as
Mercury messag

ed with his
daily illegi

ble post-
script

s.

Animals

staring through
their artifi

cially confin
ing habitat

s though al
ways most natur

ally-dressed
may wonder at

our change
ably coloring

modes of self-
expressive

ness.

Did Weinberg

become a Christ
ian at-the-end

because of his
wife's concern

ing say-sos
or (perhaps)

because he'd
"always felt

God's presence"
and desired

His time-contin
uing counten

ance.

Do Weinberg'

s slow move
ment ending

s imply a re
conciliation

with his un
bearable suffer

ings a spirit
ual acceptance

of lasting
(and musical)

strengths
and solitude

s.

For some

words have be
come a mean

s of hidden-
refuge from e

nemied danger-
zone

s.

Does Weinberg'

s loss of a
true-homeland

of person and
place soul

him with a
loneliness

of irretriev
able beauty.

Indecision

Signs warped-
through with

time-telling
truths two-

direction
ed him far

beyond his un
certain length-
of-view.

As if he

could become
reinhabit
ed with "a
fresh start"
(as they call
it) after
such-a-loss
and in the
closing time
s of his a
ging year
s.

Only when

looking-back
becomes a
sensing-for
ward does
life path it
self even bey
ond those dark
ly-wooded in
terlude
s.

Can religion (2)

a) oft routined

to a time-set

pattern re
route some from

those unpre
pared off-balan

cing God-immer
sing moment

s.

b) or are the

forms that

faith has so-
clothed it

self but hidd
en doors to

our most in
dwelling

person.

When freedom

becomes an
unlimited

call to what
ever you want

to do your
self out.

Out-figuring

We couldn'
t "figure-her-

out" perhaps
s because

she'd always
s remained an

enigma to her
own mirror

ing self-re
flection

s.

Milkweed'

s air-free
flight but

ever-so-
lightly

wind-sound
echoing

s.

Loss so

hardened
her feature

s as if
time had been

bending her
cold-down.

Her room

became her
world died

at that
very-place

no-wheres-
else.

The moon e

ven at its
brighten

ing still
nesses a sea-

wandering
soul.

For Rosemarie

Love fashion
ed her very-

being time-
sensed

floral light-
design

s.

That same bird

It must have
been that

same bird
poised at a

heighten
ed distance

time-seclud
ing.

They walked

a life most
ly in the

same-step
rhythm

s of daily-
echoing

s.

Small bird

intimate
ly color

ing its
light-in

flection
s.

He lower *(for Thomas)*

ed his voice
to their fam

ily-homed-
sensed-famil

arity.

Chinese painting

when taste
implies an

after-sens
ed sameness.

For Chung

the last
touch of snow

melting memor
ies light-a

ware.

Out of the

indwelling
darkness a

finely-felt
snow touched

these vacant
fields fresh

ly-awaken
ed.

Street

lights early

morning's
only remain

ing voice
watchful

ly-aware.

Skeletal

branches in
tensely gripp

ed with win
ter's wind-

chilling
call.

When each (2)

a) had staked-

out their own

special claim
s there re

mained noth
ing left to

divide except
that wanton

need-for-more.

b) When the wan

dering seed
s wind-releas

ed left be
hind only

those dried-
out remain

s as candle
s waxed-down

to but a
flameless

intent.

These fine

ly-veined
leaves left

the impress
ion of a pre-

routed de
sign.

Vermont

once symbol
of an independ

ent defiant-
will now

drugged-down
with the i

maginery
dreams of a

numbed-con
sciousness.

This land

seems in
waiting breath

ed-down to a
late winter

ed stillness.

Ukraine

a divided
land with less

than a scant
historical

past birth
ed anew as

unidentical
twins separ

ately apart.

Pussy-willow

a pulsing
freshly through

winter-abandon
ing touched-

pleasure
s.

Is sleep

more like
these time-de

scending
ground-depth

s immersed
in ever-dark

ening fore
boding

s.

That tree

early-March
ed bared

from the in
sistency of

winter's un
availing

sapless
claim

s.

Can time be

measured
by this road'

s prevailing
sound-length

s.

A small cera

mic bowl de
signed by

the fragran
ces of its

flowered
delicacie

s-of-touch.

For Rosemarie'

s subdued way
intimately

self-confin
ing as the

pastel blue
of this early-

timed spring
morning.

A great

power's bottom-
ground remain

s incessant
ly land-hung

ry.

A bird at

the height of
wingèdly-en

circling
those infin

ite realm
s of cloud-

spacing
s.

Indigenous

war-chant
s passion

ately enthus
ed tidal blood-

swells.

Snail's

hollowed-
out shell emp

tied of its
reclusive

ly inhabit
ing time-re

fuge.

Are conclu

sive poetic
cadence

s more-like
the land-fold

ings of its
rhythmical

ly self-sus
taining

source.

If he

"never grew
old" why had

time slowed-
him-down to

the measur
ed steps of

such a faint
ly-echoing-

resolve.

Empty-handed

He never
felt so empty-

handed as when
there was noth

ing left to
read except

the window
ed distance

s measuring-
out the length

of his self-
enduring time-

span.

He feared

those ever-re
curring sympt

oms ran out
as rats from

their bottom-
ground hole

s to inhabit
the almost-

all of his own
unrelenting

darkly-sensed
night-timed

person.

Objects (6)

a) Dr. Schimpf'

s round-eyed
owl's wisdom-

ed his
early morning

yet time-sus
pending intui

tive look-out
s.

b) A room of

Charles' paint
ings hung-

through-the-
night seemed

as alive as
their still-

coloring
brush-felt a

wakening
s.

c) Her rain-

drop earing
s suspend

ing a time-
complacent

imitative
contemplat

ion.

d) These night-

enduring tree
s seemed mot

ionless
ly called-

out of their
dream-respons

ive reverie
s.

e) Hill-hung-

houses time-
intending

the apparent
sameness of

their self-
assuming ap

pearance
s.

f) He suit-

cased his
daily person

into careful
ly amended

note-book
ing their

blank-hold
carry-

ons.

This late-

wintered
soul-drift

ing snow
seemed almost

as an imagin
ery lost-

timed season-
of-the-mind.

He feared

that timeless
day his care

fully-kept
diary would

be left blank-
ly unopen

ed.

A bird

less sky in
habited only

by sound
less snow-

calling
s.

This fine

ly-sensed
snow-down

ed an appar
ent sky-imi

tative mirr
oring.

Darkly encom

passing night
s a no-ways-

out imbedded
in those un

touchably-a
wakening-

fears.

An empty

roomed innum
erable doors

leading in
to the unknown

depth of space
d silence

s.

A bottom

less snake-fath
omed lake

d beyond the
reach of its

imagined
touch-length.

This window

ed street
watching

through its
soundless

night-voice
s.

When dream

s depth in
to their

timeless
ly lost ap

pearance
s.

Ancient

Greek church
es sunken-

down into
centurie

s of an e
ver-present

living-God.

Family-

trees increas
ingly branch

ing-out the
very urge of

a childless
present.

Woodpecker

hammering
right-rhythmi

cally in-to
the numbed

core of this
tree's winter

ed inertia.

A knock-at-

the-door late-
at-night ans

wering only
echoing

fears.

Balconie

s seemed more-
like modern

out-posts
bird-imitat

ing poised-
recalling-in

terval
s.

Through (5)

a) those escap

ing shadow

s they fled
the crocodile'

s shallowed
water's raw

ed flesh-a
waitings

blood-stream
ed carcass

ed-remain
s.

b) Man animall

ed to those
killer death-

instinct
ual now-or-

never life-
or-death

primitive
ly origin

s.

c) They shot-

them-down
trembling

Jewed-line
s into the o

pen pits of
their death-

eyed precis
ion.

d) "And the

rest was si
lence" only

those shovell
ed-depth

blood-stain
ed cries re

mained time
lessly-aloud.

e) Only that

half-forgott
en tainted i

mage of a
better-being

remains rever
ently untouch

ed Christ-
like.

This solemn

morning as
those still-

dormant tree
s hung-down

with the
weight of per

petuating
fears.

The loss-of-

love is like
a world naked

ly unbound to
its origin

ed beginning
s.

Half-personed

He half-per
soned his

father so re
cognizably

samed yet at
times so in

distinctly
otherwise as

if veined and
fleshed from a

remotely differ
ent specie

s.

Curtained

Her world
curtained be

hind color
less façade

s that kept
her almost

complete
ly protected

from her own
endemic fear

s.

Can sport

s momentar
ily body-us

into those
open realm

s of a sky-
deceiving

likeness.

Those so-

called "moral
spokesmen"

have mostly
clean-vested

their launder
ed past into

neat piles of
appropriate

sayings nice
ly-placed

linen-scent
ed.

A dense

fog left this
world as if

hidden from
its true-self

phantomed
to another

time-and-place
untouchably-

unrealized.

"You haven't

changed these
20 years" they

said though
others from-

his-class
couldn't e

ven recognize
that self-

same person.

Otherwise

At first
space ceased

to inhabit
its usually

steadfast
distance

s until e
ven his own

image blurr
ed indistin

ctly other
wise.

He felt him

self at sea
alone on an

emptied raft
drifting the

waves far-bey
ond their

timeless pre
sence.

Centenary

Dug-in down
to the blood-

felt depth
s of a contin

ually motion
less war.

At-the-end

death-bedded
to where

time began
floating past

his still ir
retriev

able pre
sence.

She lived-

a-life-of-
picture

s only place
s seldom per

soned beyond
her snap-

shot existen
ce.

For Neil

who remember
s so-much-

more of my
past that it

may have be
come his for-

the-living-it-
through.

Poet's pen

The perfect-
feel of this

touch-down
pen rounded

to the inclu
siveness of

that inwritt
en poem.

The poet'

s curtained
time-defin

ing place
windowed to-

the-length of
increasing

distance
s.

With the pale

early-March sun
still search

ing for its
light-depth

and the modest
ly innocent

snow-drops
and crocus

low-ground
ing an oncom

ing spring's still
scarcely-awar

ed presence.

"Count-your-

blessings"

they call it
though the

pains came so
strong so in

tense color
ing the whole

of her bodied-
mind that she

stopped count
ing at all

though the num
bers continual

ly kept-on-com
ing as if from

a self-perpetua
ting cause.

The "coming-

of age" less
ens that clos

ing-in space-
scope that

each step
seems almost

worlds-apart.

Weinberg

though bodied-
down with age

and disease
composed until

the very-end
of his blood-

line rhythm
ic-impulse

s.

When for

some a less-
vacant chair

becomes the
only world

left to hold-
in their

time-diminish
ing thought

s.

When the

unassuming

colors of a
tiny bird'

s flutter-
down wing

s a hope
a message in

decipherab
ly there.

a) Was Breughel'

s chain-down
monkey more

a symbol of
his own dan

gerously un
relenting

need-for-es
cape.

b) Was Goya'

s dark-threat
ening dog

his own in
stinctual

desire for
getting-above-

time's exaust
ing claim

s.

He had his-

own-way so
often that

at-the-end
there seem

ed nothing
left but a

no-ways-
out.

Faint i

mages-on-glass
as if a dimin

ishing echo
s of words

scarcely-
brought-to-

mind.

For Rosemarie

who's become-
for-me that

gold-medieval-
metallical

ly emblemmed
Constance

guiding the
boats safely-

to-port.

She sat in-

the-same-room
same-place

days-on-end
her same-faded

old-fashion
ed dress but

once something
at-first-unex

pectedly-there
brightened.

How do

these half-
dead dried-

down winter
ed leaves

feel the re
freshing

claims of
spring's

through-puls
ing light.

Genealogies (4)

a) father

sperm-bank

2 mothers
brother

unknown origin.

b) a nation

unknown past

divided history
mixed languages

varied faiths
changeable flags

patriotic

c) scientists

worked to kill us

helped us to kill
our enemies

patriotic citizens
of this or that

d) Religion

earth man

big-bang
maybe a god

if so the-
way-I-want

denomination
spiritual.

Our house

once so solid
ly homed

now harsh wind
s surround

ing its cozy
thought

s embedded

deeply within.

a) A fine paint

ing only live
s again if

seen–so a
live.

b) Once-again

Seeing it
through-your-

eyes may be
realizing

one's own once-
again.

c) History

only repeat
s itself if

we can't i
magine it

otherwise.

d) That-way

If friend
s continual

ly remain
that-way may

be because
we've statued-

them to our
own self-

view.

e) Surprised

She so-surpris
ed me as an

always-wind
breathless

ly refresh
ing.

f) Double-pass

a marriage-
way of self-

succeed
ing.

Mozart Violin Concerti 3 and 4

Mozart's natur

al gift poetical
ly contrasting

with a nod
to the coy

and soulful
ly-adept form

ed.

Mozart Adagio for Violin/Orch.

richly harmoni
cally depthed

to almost
choric-enchant

ments.

Weinberg (2)

a) Weinberg'

s daily-fear
the voice had

been stilled
dried-down

to its very
source.

b) For Weinberg

the violin
had become

his father'
s special voice

d alive to
the depths of

his own impen
etrable lone

liness.

Squirrelled

even before
that clawed-

in space-
length branch

ed its decid
edly perform

ing landing-
scope.

Train-dis

tancing the
windowed-

length of
past-dissolv

ing moment
ary-find

s.

a) Do we live-

through-our-
children or

they through-
us tunnell

ed in a dark
of light-ex

posing vista
s.

b) Do blood-

lines often
spring-over

a generat
ional abyss

as this air-
borne squirrell

ed for famil
iar tree-branch

ed affinitie
s.

These dark

woods passing
through my

train's tran
sient imagin

ing myster
ious regions

not yet fully
brighten

ed-out.

Jewed-empt

ied fields of
blood and bone

their still un
recorded earth-

depth memor
ies.

On the table

impersonal

ly gloved-
hands cutting

in-to the
source of his

most-hidden
realms-of-be

ing.

Ulm spired

to a transcen
dental height

of angelic
reflection

s.

Trains-track

s running
cross-route

s of indeci
pherable

thought-dir
ection

s.

Her granate

ring clasped
intricacie

s of lumin
ous dark-

shine.

For Rosemarie

Love-look at
76 enclosing

for all its
time-lessen

ing-hold the
complete

ness of an
entire world-

view.

Night

train darken
ing in the

shadows of
its time-reced

ing after-
glow.

Train

station's
cross-curr

ents shadow
ing their

irretriev
able busi

ness.

Mila

four-finger
ed a blond-

apparent
presence of

a world i
magined book

and touch-
wise.

Notary-

public adroit
ly paragraph-

person(ed) a
cute aware

ness of where
they might be

misleading
us around in

scrutably
blind-corner

s.

Train com

ing-in snake-
like a Jaffin-

poem to its
pre-determin

ing station
ed-premise

s.

Squirrel'

s route thin
ly-adroit to

its lithely-
instinctive

claim
s.

Was Weinberg'

s close lipp
ed attentive

ness inborn-
imitative

or because of
the system'

s watching-
out every

false-move.

a) Are leafed-

tree's winter
ed-nakedness

mirroring
a constant re

minder of
Adam and Eve'

s self-reveal
ing natur

al human
condition.

b) Vanitas

Has she be
come clothed

in the prett
ied-design

s of disguis
ing her own

most-intimate
intention

s.

Webern Bagatelles (for string quartet)

intervall
ed to a space

ful conson
ance.

Beethoven op. 18,3 *(Quartet)*

his own

(though not
heroically)

voiced close
to his classi

cal master
s.

Schumann op. 41,1 *(3)*

a) Quartet 1st mvt.

repetitous
ly stagnant-

still too rhy
thmically

self-intent
could have

learned-more
from the read

ily-moving-
on Haydn.

b) scherzo

Beethovenian
horse-trotted

aimed just-
rightly.

c) slow mvt.

Schumann

at-his-ro
mantically

best-fanta
sied world.

Frost-night

s warmed-day
s on-and-

off person
ed not quite

readily-a
daptable.

Birds

wired to an
available

sit-down at
tentive

ness.

She

always sur
prised (per

haps mostly
herself)

part-and-par
cel of her

own allusive
short-timed

nature.

Book cover

ings the al
lusive-touch

of their
word-remem

brance.

This bright

self-apparent
spring-day

cleared him
of all those

threaten
ing night-

timed impost
ures.

Self-halved

And when the

Good Lord will
ed it other

wise than his
own divided

him right-down-
the-middle

self-halved.

City Museum instrument collection (10)

a) strange

Asian instru
ments so color

fully ornament
ed that they

touch-sounded
alive by sim

ply appearing
exotically-

unheard.

b) Chalcedon

blue-skied
an almost

inevitably
appealing

vastness.

c) Heart-beat

drum-chanting
African self-

arousing dark
nesses.

d) finely tin

gled touch-

sounding
reveried

mood-enchant
ments.

e) Music-lesson

s sensually-
awakening

depth-accord
s.

f) Danced rhy

thms swaying
gently into

the ensuing
darkness

of touched-
silence

s.

g) Brass-instru

ments insist
ently present

ing blown-up
cheeked-pro

gression
s.

h) Western

orchestral-
sounding

a unity of
samed-down

instrument
al-aware

ness.

i) Bird-song

s never off-
keyed their

self-intuned
voice-familiar

colorfully-
repeating

in-calls.

Rediscover

ing the rari
fied climate

of the poem'
s subtly es

caping form
s an unchar

tered island
emerging

the midst of
an untamed o

ceaned-ex
panse.

Persistent

ly mapping-
out two-side

s to the
same terrain

animal-in
voking resist

ant war-claim
s.

When work-

routine (as
often with

the late Wein
berg) assumes

the artificial-
guise of a

spontaneous-
renewal.

For Helen

Near-death-ex
perience poet

izes the hea
venly source

of our-own
down-below

earthy word-
claim

s.

Classical

ly holding-
fast to that

creative-ten
sion between

an unnamed
self-reveal

ing source
and the craft

ed designs
of its myster

iously with
holding-pre

sence.

If "one-

thing-leads-to
another" it'

s the creat
ive prescrib

ing of a gem-
like continu

ity.

However-much

the birth-act
preforms us

in parental-
union or the

free-will of
being brought-

up to the use of
daily

parental dis
guise?

For George

The creative-
mind's as in

tricately
multi-sourced

as the nour
ishing demand

s of our-own
blood-veined

stature.

Saying-it-

less can mean-
it-more

as Haydn's
space-encom

passing a
dagios.

Even as

Christ fully-re
deemed a world

beyond-our-own
mind's i

maginatively
pre-seems its

mirroring-sub
limitie

s.

The simple

wind-evolv
ing flight of

an ordinary
bird calls-

to-mind what'
s coloring

far beyond
its-own daily-

reach.

The plastic-

abstract
monumental

ity of Gauguin'
s "Where are

you going" star
ing into a

space-perspect
ive of time

lessly unheard
silence

s.

Weinberg'

s chordal
close-down

density a
war-intens

ing deadly-
sensed time-

closure.

Labyrinthed

He became
so closed-in

on himself
as a caged-

tiger's no-
ways-out laby

rinthed.

When words

started coming-
down an indelib

le 3am black
board's no-ans

wers-left than
spelling-them-

out rightly.

Perched-on

an irretriev
able-pedestal

as a prettied-
bird artific

ally-colored.

Time's runn (3)

a) ing-out of a

nowheres-

place catch
ing-up

breathless
ly.

b) A pause

a timeless
vacancy of

there-and-
only-now.

c) A turn a

round that no-
wheres-but-now

blind-corner
ed him speech

lessly death-
like.

Near-death

experienc
ed a well

phantomed
deeper than

time's irre
trievable

stop-watch.

Why had

he been so
protective

ly knife-
wombed to such

a bloodied-
end.

Had Webern

breathless
ly spaced

the atonal
ity of newly-

sensed time-
sequence

s.

Early Webern quartets

when then line
s overlap in

to waves of
silently ex

posing densit
ies.

Relapse in

to those cool
ed-down wind-

perpetuat
ing closely-

held instinct
ual resistan

ces.

The innate

leaf-transpar
encies of a

momentary
touchless

timed-va
cancy.

A life of a

self-conceal
ing withdraw

al into a
mirrored

appearance-
sake.

Marin Marais' (3)

a) darkly sugg

estive tone

s at the viol
s lower-levell

ed their sound-
sweeping depth

s.

b) an almost

Brahmsian

soul-length
colored-

intonation.

c) shortly-a

dept dance-

phased alter
nating rhy

thmic-inter
vals.

A warning a

gainst creating

others in one'
s own image

an only one-
time godly

self-express
iveness.

Uli Hoeness

FC Bayern's
one-and-only

swelling in
full-time ac

clamation
s rode the

irresistib
le waves

wind-surfing
his over-

wrought self-
image.

Such over-car

ing sweet tone
s those fad

ing softly di
minishing

colors pink-
and-lilac

strawberr
ies-and-cream.

Happy-ending

usually left-

him with that
ever-so-sooth

ing music's
time-emptied

phrasing
s.

5 classmates (5)

a) L. G.

She became so
incisively

critical
like cutting

paper in-to
little-lost-

heaps of self-
selective

momentary-
impulse

s.

b) Danny B.

as flashy
as his loud-

mouthed op
portunely

red-haired
visually

self-accom
ating presence.

c) M. M.

a lesser-
salesman of

a personal
ity-type

always out
for more good-

byes self-en
during acclaim

s.

d) Robert

a quiet-type
took to the

fields of
touch-sound

ing-imagin
ed color

ings.

e) Danny R.

at his friend
ly height

seldom look
ed-down on

his lesser
time-equival

ent class-
mates.

St. Francis (2)

a) Did St. Fran

cis language

a bird-mean
ing sense

or did they
understand

not what he
said but

what he'd be
come.

b) That hungri

ed wolf tamed
to a confess

ional speech-
down demean

or.

For Rosemarie

Your modest-
beauty contin

ually tame
s that hung

ried-wolf-of-
mine.

Boeing 777 (12)

a) disappeared

without record

of when-where-
why 239 passen

gers either at
the bottom of

the Indian O
cean or held-

hostage in
some distant

and remote
land What happ

ened to them
at that

irretriev
ably lost-mo

ment.

b) Missing per

son never re
turned after

the war last
seen by none

of his com
rades killed

at the dis
tant sight of

Moscow Decem
ber 1941.

c) lived with

a stolen pass

became a
nother person

(learned his
role well)

Jew-star bur
ied at the

depth of his
bloodied-con

science.

d) His memory

gone his per
son unsourced

a distant
dialect left

for the spec
ialists to re

locate that
remotely

lost-person.

e) The last she

remembered
her name

dimly time-
written on

all-encom
passing-dark

nesses.

f) Last heard

of in the
midst of the

Pacific O
cean thous

ands of mile
s adrift

from a home
and self

they never re
turned to.

g) Space explor

ers lost-touch
with their

home-base
somewhere

s out-there
spaceful

ly in-search
of-a-nowhere

s-else.

h) Even as a

child he mapp
ed-off the

boundarie
s to his

(as yet) un
discovered-

world rarely
fear-stepped

beyond that
limited-con

fine.

i) Those frail

little-grade-
school-girl

s innocent
ly hop-scotch

ing their
touch-down

chalk afore
that fear

some hell-
marked end.

j) When the

dark of that
unremember

ed tunnel e
choing his

self-escap
ing shadow

s.

k) One read of

her later
that lithe-

blond pony-
tailed nine-

year-old-
girl blood-

found in a
remotely-wood

ed-enclos
ure.

l) However-much

she tried
couldn't find

her way home
lost in a

labyrinth
of self-en

tangling
fear

s.

March 18 2014

(7 Poems for Rosemarie's 76th birthday) (7)

a) Sun-shine

city's full
of brightly

displayed un
timed forget

fulness.

b) As if this

world began
with your

dreamily
soul-trans

cending blue-
timed smile.

c) Fields of

spring-time
flowers trans

parently
light-aspir

ing.

d) When souther

ly winds ever-
so-softly-

touched with
souled-express

iveness.

e) Shadowless

ly brighten
ed with Monet'

s wind-expan
sive light-

vision
s.

f) These time-

awakening
rivers-of-the-

mind landscap
ing untouch

ed-myster
ious-silenc

es.

g) A world-of-

just-two
self-enclos

ing realm
s of an

only-now bey
ondness.

Webern 1909 *(for Tony)*

Intervall
ed spaced-

out sound-in
tensities

a newly appar
ent sense-of-

conscious
ness.

Images (12)

a) ever-so-

graceful

ly form-in
creasing

imagined-a
wareness

es.

b) Momentary-

light's

soundless-
inflect

ions.

c) The feel-

of-silk's
hand-increas

ing form-
flow.

d) Sound-impress

ions shadow
lessly space-

confining.

e) Sea-salt-

taste finger'

s evasive
sand-sensed

refinerie
s.

f) Mood-shad

owings a
moonless

ly obscur
ing-night.

g) Wooded en

closure'
s myster

ious indwell
ings.

h) A cat'

s secretly
soundless-

intent paw-
length

s.

i) The blood

call-depth
s of night-

feared imag
ination

s.

j) When the

depth-well'

s echoing-
down mediev

al sound-
wave

s.

k) Love's

self-circ
ling touch-

found guard
ed-interior

s.

l) That rose-

depth kiss
of tidal

self-immers
ions.

Hebrides Ouverture *(Mendelssohn)*

Wave-sound
s spaceful

ly pursuing
their persist

ently aroused
watered-in

stinct
s.

His face

so impenetra
bly fixed

right-down
to the depth

s of all-my-
own death-call

ings.

2nd Piano Concerto (Saint-Saëns)

He learned
his lesson

s well All
the right ro

mantic cliché
s power-work

finger-finer
ies withall

without where
mind-lyrical

substance
truly sustain

s.

Scottish Symphony (Mendelssohn) (2)

a) Mood-tonali

ties as the

shifting-
light of dark-

ly escap
ing dance-in

terval
s.

b) Timed-land

scaping
s rhythmic

ally awaken
ed from their

imaginative
ly source-

intuned ori
gins.

Once in the

midst of a
vastly encom

passing ocean
he imagined

he'd been
living in the

remembran
ce of those

rarely deciph
erable lost

time-sequenc
es.

If the end'

s as the be
ginning of

conscious
ly-involving

darkly-sensed
illusion

s.

This early-

spring sun'
s growth those

living seed
s of time'

s continual
earth-bound

renewal
s.

Orchestral (4)

a) over-sounds

the reflect

ive touch-
sense of spac

ed intimac
ies.

b) Chamber

music room
s those most-

personal inter
vals of con

templative
voiced-trans

parencie
s.

c) Wallace Stevens'

"Two Letters"
me into

those quiet re
frains of a

no-wheres-o
ther-than.

d) If one can'

t imitate si
lence then

let-it-speak
through its

own over-hear
ing presence.

The nimble

echoing-quick
ness of foot

step's bare
ly ground-

touched.

Over-

sight bird
s envision

ing those
rarely unspok

en realm
s of heaven

ly-expanse.

a) Walt Whitman'

s pantheist
ic-self as god-

like as the o
cean's incess

antly tidal o
vercoming

s.

b) for my part

I'd take the

simplicity
of overheard

silence
s those mo

mentary touch
ed-awareness

es to all of
his over-runn

ing repetitive
chronical

s his stuck-
needle's voic

ed self-indulg
ences.

c) One poem

that Lincoln-
dirge would

have been e
nough if cut-

down 400 time
s to its vi

tal essence.

d) babble

babble babb

le suffocat
ing the lang

uage with his
overwrought

swelling hyper
boles of sen

sual exhibit
ionism.

Has night be

come the time
less sleep

of sensing
those unvoic

ed restful-
calling

s Or is it
a phantom

ed awareness
downed to the

depths of a
bottomless

deep.

A lone

house seclud
ed on a voice

less slop
ing into

realms of un
inhabited

silence
s.

Wintered

trees naked
ly ashamed

of their stripp
ed-down all-

but abandon
ed bareness

es.

A lone un

used road lead
ing into

those wooded
darkness

es of an all-
encompass

ing no-ways-
out.

These feel-

through soft
nesses of

pussy-willow'
s stream-

lined puls
ings.

First-sens

ed spring flo
wers seem as

if primarily
touched with

their own
self-accomat

ing coloring
s.

(and) if you

could read

these initial
ly tentative

lines to an o
therwise

rightly-ex
tended ex

pressive
ness.

He called it

"stop" right-

there only-
then in a no-

wheres of
breathless

ly-held dis
tancing

s.

Window-shelved

Why these i
maginary cac

tus deserted
to their lone

inquench
able thirst

ings.

That-way

If he couldn'
t see or e

ven feel-it
that-way

off-tracked
from all his

interior re
sonance.

Stigmatized

a single
off-color

rose review
ing its-own

untouched
selved-be

ing.

Window-shelv

ed appearanc
es a frieze-

review of
most-unlike

ly (if less
companion

able) siloue
ttes.

Circe-callings

Her intend
ing smile left

persistant sha
dowings of his-

own self-re
luctant

desiring
s.

These bird

s seem air-
freeing the

wings of this
early-morning

spring-light.

Fields-of-

sound wind-es
caping the

levelled-
reach of their-

own ground-
persuasion

s.

"First-come

first-serve"
but not alway

s with word
s finding-

into their
pre-ordained

expressive
ness.

One can't

live the fail
ed-life of

others pull
ing-down in

to their ir
retriev

able time-
gloom.

Being-satis

fied with one'
s own inescap

able-self can
create a stead

ied inertia
of mind-and-

soul.

For Caspar David

Friedrich the
moon may have

symbolized
Christ's God-

reflective
light as if

it hadn't also
been sourced

in His own
self-being.

When a young

East-Ukrain
ian of Russ

ian-speaking
parents ask

ed of his
true-identity

only a sus
tained over

heard silence
as an ever-

lasting re
sponse.

Haydn'

s early violin
concerti ro

bustly sound-
creating an

imperative
need for a

self-defining
finalized

form-sense.

Change-of

weather
ing a cloud-

consuming
heaven's in

terior self-
enclosure

s.

A black-sk

ied bird's
shadowless

ly self-de
fining iden

tity.

Schubert's last quartet D 887 (first mvt.) (2)

a) Is that real

ly Schubert
exploring the

intervals of a
nother-side-to-

self-open-field
s a dramatic

questioning
the where of

being so
found-out.

b) Repetition

s can long
outdo their

course as
coins worn-

down from
extra-usage.

Slow mvt. (2)

a) souled-back

to those ly

rical self-
interior

s.

b) Dramatic

turbulenc

es can sea-
sick even

the most
steadfast

of self-com
posure

s.

Deep in (4)

a) to the tree'

s bark-smooth

ed-length
the rains soak

ed secret
ly time-encom

passing dark
ness.

b) Its branch

es beholden
to a sap-en

during stren
gth.

c) Its leaf

less memorie
s the reach

ing depth
of a stone-

down lake.

d) (and yet)

it still-stood
a vacancy of

timeless
self-endur

ance.

"Let's just

forget that"
he said as

if time would
n't always be

hearing its
still-echoing

resonance
s.

Friendships *(for Neil) (12)*

a) is driving-

through a

blinding snow-
storm with

an old-down
car of thread-

bare tires
just-to-meet.

b) for George of

being sourced
for that same

creative-fi
bre.

c) for Hans Z.

same-God
same-place

being fully
self-intuned.

d) for Ingo

on that late
summer Starn

berger See
your boat glid

ing-past our
same eye-ex

tending curr
ents.

e) for Warren

being phrased
to a wordful

sense of intri
cately-depth

ed-meaning
s.

f) for Chung

a more-than-
common sensi

bility finely
samed-attun

ed.

g) for Thomas

familied-togeth
er to a Claud

ius-like indiv
iduality.

h) for Lenore

as if art and
word could

become so
personally

interwoven.

i) for "S. L."

s dialectic
friendship

tensioned
to a common

meeting-ground.

j) for Hani

who still re
mains elusive

ly otherwise.

k) for Martin

churched
to a criti

cal time-ask
ing venture.

l) for Michael P.

with his so
friendly (e

ven gentle)
self-standing

poise.

The shade

less bonsai
tree poetical

ly circling
its own self-

enclosing in
tricate shadow

ings.

Silk dream

s immersed
her in those

soft gentle
waves of mid-

light compass
ion.

Spitzweg's

artificial
ly medieval-

romantical
ly provincial

back-drop
s his tongue-

in-cheek semi-
apparently

fairy-tale-
like no-where

s-place
s.

Would Shakes

peare still-
have-signed

his name in
11 different

ways even a
fter Dr. John

son inhabited
the language

with his-own-
only do-it-

my-ways.

Such astute *(for Warren)*

"classical"
grammar may

have ordered
the myster

ious range
of poetical

ly self-con
cealing corri

dors in-to
lines of uni

formly dress
ed school-child

ren patient
ly awaiting

their daily-
consuming

food-ration
s.

Cool-drop-

holding rain'
s incessant-

need for its
insistent

ly self-ex
pressive

ness.

Jealousy

Why must
you celebrate

those self-en
closing dream

s-of-yours
foreign to

my own in-
folding

ternderness
es.

Aging couple

s dancing
their Shakes

pearian-Guardi
an heritage

into echo
ing shadow

s of a time
lessly appar

ent youthful
ness.

Beethoven'

s greatly-ori
ginal First

Rasumovsky Quar
tet so double-

lengthed Haydn'
s intrinsical

ly concise
classical form

(ing) a new
emotional-

relevance a
mening me

four-or-five
times-over.

Leaveless

patterns of
wintered

shadowing
a vacancy

of their
still-impend

ing time-
need

s.

That existen

tially-adept
sermon left me

feeling "no
better than my

father"'s own
self-deceiving

ways.

Over-sized

birds holding
the heaven

s down to
their weighted

land-assumpt
ions.

Blood-test

ing too close
ly to our

own self-con
cealed life-

processing
s.

Passion-time

snow clouds
darkly conceal

ing the whiten
ed puritie

s of His
bloodied-effu

sions.

Schubert' (2)

a) s A minor

sonata D. 743

tensioned
at the very

interior
of his self-

poetic being
a hymn on life

and beauty
ever-darkly

dramatical
ly-threaten

ed.

b) No repetit

ive amens need
ed here a

completed
sense of the

most personal
of question

ings and in
tuned-response.

Invasion

of birds tower
ing the hea

vens darkly
phrasing.

Snow-down

s sloping
these vacant

ly-express
ive-hills

soothing
ly cool-sens

ed.

Late winter-

interludes i
magining a

Schubert
ian theme

still haunt
ingly-timed.

Boeing 777

black-box at
the bottom-

of-the-ocean
drifting an

untold depth
ed-mystery of

its unexplain
able disappear

ance.

Dowland

achieved the
height of his

fame-silenc
ed from those

most intimate
of lyrical

accord
s.

Spring

blossomed
the Chinese

painter
s to a cele

brating-time
of self-re

newal.

The Pacifica

Quartet's
cellist seem

ed like cross-
eying where-

tone could act
ually be call

ed-out.

Quartet 2 (Britten)

After the un
touchable per

fection of a
Haydn op. 76

one could ask
whether form

isn't a pre-
given sense

for ordering
time and

space.

For Corinne and Tom

Landslide

at Washington
State the

scenic beauty
so took-hold

of their per
soned-being

cascading-
down to the

depths of an
inpenetra

ble chasm.

Dying just-

rightly may
become a call

ing-back to
life's time-

telling se
quence

s.

Good doctor

s poised mid-
way between

I'm-you-
down-there

and a distanc
ed-proficien

cy of a
truly-craft

ed-intention.

Wishful-

thinking has
often become

a life-line
holding-

tight to a
time-seeking

depth.

Too-near to

death to deny
its still

prime-sensed
motivation.

Considering

his-own-self-
importance

he often allow
ed others to

pay-for his
still outstand

ing-bill
s.

Light-heart

ed may often
help take-the-

weight-off of
some of those

pre-intending
daily-press

ures.

On my poetry

If the line
s don't keep-

moving who
else could be

called for
keeping-them

in-place.

As they cut-

the-woods-
down its in

brooding dark
nesses came

flying-out
wingèd-for a

lasting self-
protection.

Those steadfast

ly indiffer

ent to the
suffering

of others
may die as a

statued lone
liness to a

one-man cause.

a) Pain

screams
voiceless

ly louder.

b) Not

the-impact-
of-stone

scarcely e
choing.

c) The mid-day

sun untouch
ably there.

d) Birds distan

cing higher
soundless

ly apparent.

e) His heart

(if it was
his) mutely

vacant.

f) Has time

slowed-down
to its death

ed near
ness.

g) A pain so

intense

that not e
ven prayer

could be si
lently awaken

ed.

h) Gesualdo'

s Maundy Thurs
day densely

self-inhabit
ing.

i) Haydn's 7

Last Words
as if that

distance
between

voice and
sound time-

suspend
ing.

He could

only believe
in the "holy

Christian
church" when

it would
stop trying

ever-so-hard
to believe

in itself.

a) Centuries

long under the
heavenly Cross

they crucifie
d His first-

beloved peo
ple.

b) Had Jew-

starred be

come the in
delible-sign

of His last
ing-chosen

ness.

A Winter's Tale *(Shakespeare) (5)*

a) The King of

Sicily more a
pre-formed

Othello with
out the grad

ual design
s of a slow

ly disinte
grating love-

faith.

b) An imaginat

ive happy-end
ing plot that

leaves one un
happily dissatis

fied with its
artificial

two-part trag
ic-comedy.

c) Can one real

ly imagine
kissing a

paint-drip
ping beauty

brought-back-
to-life's out

framed tender
nesses.

d) Only the dense-

Shakespear
ian language

can partly
veil its too-(two)

themed-said
with too

little sub
stancial

ly-involving-
depth.

e) Are blood-

ties (then)

the real es
sence (not

upbringing)
of a truly

aristocrat
ic demeanor.

Brockes Passion *(Keiser 1712) (5)*

a) The shorten

ed simplici
ty of saying

(more?) by u
sing less.

b) Arias less-

swollen than
those of High-

Baroque.

c) Those al

most airy solo-
themes spac

iously com
pelling.

d) Brockes

a fine nature-
poet here

vastly physi
cally over-

stating the
theme's emot

ionalized im
pact.

e) Inbetween

Schütz's
truly biblical

ly-depthed trans
parencie

s and Bach'
s overwhelm

ing express
ive-faith.

Unequal Marriage (Leibl)

Her young

shapely-bod
ied eye

s deceptive
ly same-dir

ectioned
as his wrink

led self-satis
fying hungr

ied instinct
s.

If (as some

maintain) sell
ing-one's-body'

s different
from selling-

ones-soul'
s a bodiless

unpersoned
self-being.

Intimacies (10)

a) After Shakespeare

An island-
world self-

enclosed
so familiar

that each
word become

s as but-a-
touch of that

most-intim
ate-place.

b) For Rosemarie

When your
voice become

s lowered
as moon-lit

shadows to
but secluded

silently-with
holding whis

pering
s.

c) When Haydn

pianissimo

s those un
touched-revela

tions of his
inspoken

space-tonali
ties.

d) As a fisher

playing those
darkly-sensed

waters to the
very-depth of

his own self-
evasive silen

ces.

e) Those moment

s of only

here-and-now
as if time

suspending
its light-

spaceful call
ings.

f) When prayer

becomes the

shadowing
s of a voice

less respon
se.

g) When mother

lit those Fri

day-night
candles into

my own child
ful remembran

ces.

h) Return

ing home
from those in

vasive city-
sounds to

one's own
voiceless

quiet.

i) The presuming

innocence

of Charles Ed
ward Ives' pre-

World-War-I
rural-Ameri

can quiet
udes.

j) The still-

life of George
s de la Tour'

s Christ-like
candled-pre

sence.

If there

only could-
have-been a

more Christ-re
ceptive-glad

ness to bibli
cal protest

ant's so ser
iously-inten

sed self-sha
dowing

s.

For Rosemarie

when the fab
riced-color

s of your
dress match

your-own
self-intun

ing smile
s.

Pre-cursor

s Marx Darwin
Freud of the low

er-level-man
deprived of

love spirit and
soulled (sold) -

down to those
underground

World-War-I
dehumanized

pits.

Van Gogh (6)

a) Starry Night (1888)

's unity or an
all-consuming

shimmering
light heaven

ly-sourced.

b) The bridge of Langlois in Arles (1888)

symmetric

ally time-with
holding an

almost ether
ial light

ness.

c) The Sower (1888)

darkly field
ed time-e

merging per
sonalized

light-source.

d) Self Portrait (1887)

Two-color
ed eyeing the

turbulent
depth of a

deeply-troubl
ed soul.

e) Olive Tree (1889)

s ecstatic
ally trembl

ing their dis
embodied

soul-reach.

f) Willows at Dawn (1888)

as if their
colored-

form had been
sun-called

innocent
ly awaken

ed.

Gauguin (4)

a) Good Morning
Monsieur Gauguin (1889)

mysterious
ly fenced in a

distantly-e
voking time-

flow.

b) Tahiti Idyllic (1901)

free-circling
that blood-en

closured un
touchable

holiness.

c) Tahiti Pastoral (1893)

as if that
touching-

flute awaken
ed the rhythm

ic-source of
coloring-

dance.

d) Les Alyscamps
(Arles 1888)

as if this
landscape

had been bir
thed to its

through-color
ing indigen

ous source.

Origins (10)

a) Is color o

rigined in
the cool

light of the
moon's reflect

ive glow.

b) Are the low-

tide winds
sourced from

the sea's time-
apparent still

nesses.

c) Why have

these shadow
ing mountain

s ranged e
ven-beyond

the depth of
their all-in

clusive time
lessness.

d) even the

smallest
of bird

s birthed
with the airy-

light of wing
èd-illusion

s.

e) First flower

s wetted with
the melting

snow's seed-
sensing de

sires.

f) Why is the

sky's blue
depthed e

ven-beyond
its time-ex

panding ori
gins.

g) Can our in

candescent
love's-light

fade-down
to the can

dle's breath
less-flame.

h) You ask of

the night's
transcend

ing mask
ing the ebb-

and-flow of
the tide's e

ternally rhy
thmic persua

sions.

i) Timeless

cities may be
come ashed-

in-flame
but their

dead-voice
s speak cen

turies a
live.

j) Wind-sens

ing rivers
voiced from

their seclus
ively wooded-

confine
s.

Some painting

s (as often
with Gauguin)

colorfully
transcend

ing their organ
ic-whole.

Why do these

white-staid
houses (espec

ially when the
sun's dimmed)

seem almost
apparently-

out-used.

My father so

over-shadow
ed whomever

he met seem
ed almost e

lusively non-
apparent.

Was it the

moon cycling
her darkly-

intended sha
dowing de

sires.

a) Unspoken

silence
s resonance

their scarce
ly-echoing

untouched-en
closure

s.

b) Was it her

finely-fabri
ced dress em

bellishing
distant but

secretly with
holding in

stinct
s.

Was it the

unknown discord
s of Shakespeare'

s most-personal
life that Othello

ed him in
to the eternal

depths of such
jealousied

evil-premonit
ions.

The black-box

of that Boeing
777 bottomed

the ocean
with the ti

dal death-
cries of those

239 timeless
echoing

s.

Personality types (5)

a) The habitual-

doubter
should (per

haps) have
question

ed his own
self mirror

ing image.

b) Like a prett

ily-colored-
parrot she fea

thered herself
with the rhetor

ic of plumm
ed self-exaltat

ions.

c) The usual suck

er with noth
ing-to-lose

except his
price-lower

ing expectat
ions.

d) His farthest

imaginative
reach-of-view

left him bran
ched-in meditat

ive ecstatic
sing-song

s.

e) Pink felt

himself mystic
ally attuned

to heavenly
voices so

word-rare
that left him

equally self-
intranced.

Wishful-think

ing of a bett
er-world than

your own in
stincts could

possibly e
ver achieve

more than
word-wise.

a) Elegiac Song
(Beethoven op. 118)

as if man
had become

"too holy"
to suffer

such-a-fate
despite his

own self-per
fecting i

deals.

b) Brahms' Requiem

as biblical
as Christ him

self Only one
had been chos

en to witness
and fulfill

man's irrever
sible sin-death-

burdening
no-escape

routes.

c) Passion-time

a world dan
cing to the

death-beat
s of its own

self-reveal
ing earthy-in

stinct
s.

d) Was the Ti

tanic symbol
of a pre-World-

War-I on the
brink of sink

ing into
the nether-

world-depth
s of its own

unfathom
able hybris.

e) "Looking the

other way"

they called
it as the Jew

s herded open-
aired into

cattle-trains
fit just-right

for their pre-
determining

slaughter-
houses.

f) Humanism

they called
it stone-flow

ering the time
less grave

s of man'
s self-redeem

ing "idea of
progress".

g) To begin a

gain out of
the blood-stain

ed-rubble of
a world at

war against
God's helpless

ly-delivered
chosen-one

s.

h) As if love-

faith-and-
hope the only

message left
for a world

circling a
round that

artificial
sun of its

own self-en
closing

labyrinth.

Two Sisters (2)

a) She couldn'

t "love other
s as herself"

's unbeloved
inopportune.

b) She always

needed a refuge
an upstair

s roomed in
her own time-

impending
fears.

Bluebells

darkly-sourced
to their my

sterious
ly rising

colored-ex
pressive

ness.

Just-right

She felt her
self just-

right dress
ed in the

certained-
colors of a

satisfying
self-suffi

ciency.

Classical

ly-content
only when

those careful
ly-chosen

words suit
the inherent

needs of
their own

self-being.

For Rosemarie

(as you)
have depthed

a self-enclos
ing unity

of intimate-
expressive

ness.

My father

checkered
the drawing-

board of his
time-expand

ing life with
you-take-two

I'll-answer
three-fold.

When time e

ventually
comes-down-

on-us (as
with Uli

Hoeness)
there's litt

le-room-left
for our space

lessly endow
ed self-impri

sonings.

When even

hospital
s breeding

the hidden
germs of our

defenseless
ly-diseased

knifed-expos
ures.

Those self-

encompass
ing tonal-

depths of
Marin Mar

ais' viols
left him con

tinually color
ing-through.

Brahms Violin Sonata 1 last mvt.

Current

s of tension
uneasing the

depth-source
of a self-ex

posing equili
brium.

Alena at 12 plus

Was it her
endemical

ly-sourced
darkly-phased

mood-moon-cy
cling or the

stream-flow
of pre-adoles

cent sensibil
ities.

Aron

Better-for-
him to have

been just
left squirr

elling his
own selective

ly-branched
blithely self-

unassuming
height

s.

Butterflied (10)

a) elusive

ly netting

catchy-phra
ses color

fully-sens
ed.

b) The call of

those open-
field's sun-

vista's
timeless

ly wind-enti
cing.

c) A momentary

shift of
self-involv

ing touched-
sensibilit

ies.

d) Slow-start

gear-shift
ing space

d time-sen
sation

s.

e) As if word

s had died
in her mo

ment's dress-
coloring

s.

f) City-height

s upstand
ing the arti

ficial depth
of his shad

owless per
soning.

g) The train

densely mov
ing through

his voice
d-inflect

ions.

h) For Rosemarie

Some self-
samed path

s have word
ed-us

togeth
er spring-

timed.

i) That roof-

haunting
crow's shad

owed-fore
boding

s.

j) These flow

ers have dull
ed from their

same-sensed
light-affinit

ies.

Opportune

symphonic-
bombast

and poetic-
chantings

over-toned
most of his

refreshing
ly taste-re

ceptive word-
sensibilit

ies.

The first

leaf-green
ever-so

lightly
dressed in

its apparent
ly no-where

s from-in
habiting

now.

For Rosemarie (10)

a) Why need of

more than

those touch
ed-voice

less moment
s-of-our

s.

b) Worlds of un

told explorat
ion medieval

castles still
so-firmly-stan

ced Beethovenian
heroic-assuran

ces whereas
(for me) only

this momentary-
now of your

dressed-through
calming-pre

sence.

c) Inge (as

most at our
age) felt the

loss of a
years-long

partner an
always-there

personed
in receptive

ly-voiced ex
pressive

ness.

d) Not even

those soft
darkly-hued

strings of
a Marais'

suite could
attune us to

more of a
depthed-re

sponse.

e) A kiss that

depths even-
more of our

darkly-resound
ing soul-find

s.

f) We seem to

have been pre-
conceived

mapped-out
landscaped

to this all-
encompass

ing oneness-
of-ours.

g) These ever-

incoming sound
ful-coloring

s of the ebb-
and-flow of

our daily-rhy
thmic-shore-

finding
s.

h) Love-poem

s oft over-
do (due) the

infolding
bonds of their

increasing
life-flow

Not-this-one!

i) A world with

out you becoming
an all-consum

ing darkness
es' ever-

increasing
starless

night.

j) Your indwell

ing smile re
mains for me

that ever-
young time'

s recall
ing.

k) Even Brahms

(the classical-
romantic as

Mendelssohn)
lost much of

his youthful
ly-maturing

vitality e
ver-constant

ly renewing
what wasn't

there for his
self-indulg

ent-reaffirm
ing-freshness.

l) Whereas Haydn

and Mozart's in
dependent-

together
ness nurtured

an increas
ingly poised-

finality of
an always

cultured
depthed-ex

pressive
ness.

Mainly early-sensed remembrances (10)

a) Remember

ing the flow
ers but not

their real
names become

s still-truer
than knowing

how they're call
ed without real

izing the depth
of their scent-

form-and-intimate-
coloring

s.

b) Is it per

sons (let's
say class-mate

s) we remember
or momentary i

mages of their
fleeting

(though time
lessly) with

holding self.

c) That self-en

closing pond
on the way to

the high school
still reflect

ing my teen
age inexplicit

ly sensed-lone
liness.

d) Neil's house

secluded in
wooded self-

contentment
looms now

still distant
ly remote.

e) Virgil Thomp

son's setting
of "then he

shall be as
the light of

the morning"
still instinct

ively rising
from the dawn

of my own poet
ic sensibiliti

ies.

f) First grade

Dick and Jane
books as if

words had
sourced the

names of
their own self-

recalling color
ings.

g) My third-

grade-world
still mapped

to the ebb-
and-flow of

their tree-
lined intima

cies.

h) Summer

camp's open-
aired refresh

ingly eased
sound-flow

s.

i) I may have

feared (then)
the tunnell

ed darkness
es of my own

self-conceal
ing voice.

j) The close

ly-felt step
s to Robert'

s Old-English
house left me

with those
self-inhabit

ing touched-
echoing

s.

Slow Introductions (Haydn)

Curtain-rais
ers to

the unfathom
ed depth of a

spaciously-
encompass

ing world-
view.

Violin Concerto (Mendelssohn)

if less fibered
than the Beet

hoven or Brahm
s yet reflect

ively poetical
oceans-a

drift.

Nielsen'

s woodwinds oft
dialogued

between the
instrument'

s self-allur
ing aesthet

ic and the
performer'

s temperamen
tal irregular

ities.

The immensing *(for Tony)*

waves of Sibel
ius' darkly prim

ieval landscap
ings.

Can one call

Germany's lack
of a manner

istic phase
pre-tensed to

its prevading
expression

istic-mode.

a) Was the

18th The cen
tury for tru

ly great music
while its paint

erly counter
parts oft so

anemically
unsubstan

cial.

b) If a depthed-

understand
of poetry

balances
the word-page

with its bio
graphical

background
What should

one say of
Shakespeare

's seeming
ly-lack-of-

any.

c) Few can real

ize why Vermeer
so coolly self-

composedly Pro
testant convert

ed (perhaps for
marriage sake?)

to Catholicism.

d) If there

hadn't been
great teacher

s as Bellini
Haydn Pushkin

would we still
be lacking

those epochs
of standard-

bearing import
ance.

Marked

Achilles

healed with
that singular

weakness e
ven Goliath

fully-armed
with ridicule

could be mark
ed (as each-

of-us) to
those secret

ly hidden
wound-place

s even self e
vasive.

Is jealousy

an indigenous
temperamental

hazard (as per
haps with Shakes

peare) or pro
portioned to

the passion
ate claims of

one's own love-
sight

s.

Seeking refuge

from a world
impassioned

with an irrecon
cilable hate

may mean becom
ing increasing

ly awared to a
self-absent

sense of shor
ed-security.

Her pudgy-fudge

d smile rippl
ed with fat-

accumulat
ions.

Characters (9)

a) Far-off

places strange
ly exotic ex

periences still
persued her

provincial
ly less-compli

ant home-town-
self.

b) Miss Bartlett

a grammar
ian of the

meticulous
ly-correct

old-fashion
ed spinster

ed-school over
come (but

once) with the
summer-night'

s star-lit ex
actly puntuat

ed-correct
ness.

c) He bet his

last-change
not on the

thorough-bred
sleekness-of-

horse but on
his calculat

ing instinct
for pre-empted

price-fixing.

d) As a poetic

ally-inclined
child he felt

the ferris-wheel
ing him through

those blissful
ly awakened

realms of al
ways-oncoming

star-climbing.

e) Mr. Withers

our most-sensi
tive highly

bred-through
English-honor

s advisor Shakes
peared his cho

sen-texts with
such finerie

s of a delib
erating inner-

eyed contemplat
ion.

f) If he could

n't exclaim ex
actly the right-

word-for-it
weighted still

heavily on his
soul-immens

ing habitat
ion.

h) Tweeded-one-
could-say

He became arti
culately in-

bred (tweed
ed one-could

say) to his
mathematic

ally-correct
(even person

alized) daily-
response-hypoth

eses.

i) Those romantic

cally-enthused
young ladies

always saving
their drowning

(though deep
ly-sensitis

ed)-infatuat
ions.

j) Our school-

principal
readied his

deeply inbalan
cing chair's

feature
s set al

ways prepar
ed for the-

possibly-
worst.

Episodic (4)

a) Mr. Tew our

pleasantly-
astute history

teacher always
s expected I'

d know the-
right-answer

s even after
a week sick

ness-leave
ten minutes of

highly imaginat
ive fantasied

it-could-have-
been

s.

b) Miss Reid'

s strictly
measure

d her 4th-
grade face

d right at
your time-em

barassing
I-don't-know

s.

c) My second

grade on-stage-

appearing (as)
a run-away cow

raked with far
mer Eddie Eis

ner's catching-
on-up to his

abounding
surprise

s.

d) Armed

When necessary
keep her at-

arm's-length
or better-yet

armed in the
tenderness

of self-supp
orting pleas

ures.

It cooled

in to the
truly less-

flowering-
sense of

earth-bound
inclinat

ions.

When the ri

vers ran dry
only the cold

stones left
warming for a

distant
(though faint

ly heard)
sun-climbing.

Why expect

more than what'
s given as if

we'd been cer
tained to real

izing just-
that.

Does that

daily tree-
lined bird

amassing
such spacious

distance
s realize the

depth of its
own self-inur

ing sameness.

Is the vast

nakedness
of late autum

nal trees and
those of their

pre-spring-
time leaf-grow

th to a last unity
of timing-sense.

Only at the

end of their
mid-mountain

climb did
they realize

the height-
length of

their foot-
marked expos

ures.

Can "love-at-

first-sight"
more than a

totally self-
encompass

ing time-
swell.

She wanted-

for-words
though she'

d always
known of their

still unspok
en silence

s.

Do still-

life painting
s help us

to see what
nature had mo

mentarily
left-behind.

Caspar David

Friedrich's
moon-survival-

painting
s mounting

most myster
iously their

pre-design
ed self-inhab

iting route
s.

She left (be

hind) allusive
shadowing

s of scarce
ly uncertain

ed awareness
es.

Why did

that pre-de
signed bird

color ever-
so-faintly

my first morn
ing's poem

ed arrival-
spell.

After Charles Edward Ives

Is it those
unanswer

ed question
ings that so

allusive
ly space-us

anew.

Op. 96

Unsuspect
ing works as

Beethoven'
s last violin

sonata must
have surpris

ed his so-
oft pre-form-

defining in
stincts.

Please

don't expect
poems to

create their
own rules

but (rather
instead) a

voiced renew
al.

Brahms 3rd Quartet op. 67 last mvt.

simply ran-
out-of-breath

that toughly-
fibred-Brahms

(also) lyri
cally attuned

now sweeten
ed-trivial

ized.

Kurtág Quartet op. 28

Sound-pulsed

time-escap
ing interlude

s.

Beethoven Quartet op. 131 (3)

a) 1st mvt.

the eternal
flow of time

less sequenc
es.

b) some-timed

eccentrical

ly race-runn
ing intricate-

rhythmic laby
rinth

s.

c) (but then)

slowed in
to spiritual

ly-consuming
soul-depth

s.

He insist

ently pressed
too-hard

until the pen
finally gave-

way broke.

Gauguin

colored his
instinct

ual need not
for the e

rotic-exotic
but metaphysi

cally-sensed
distancing

s.

For Rosemarie (3)

a) Can taste be

(come) a pre-

ordained
selective-

unity of
form-sense.

b) The first-of-

green seem
s as if

birthed from
a child-like

pre-ordained
innocence.

c) Wordsworthian

Must child
ren learn to

see-shorter
than their

wide-eyed in
tuition

s.

Are the Rocke

fellers and Carne
gies (as Willa

Cather insist
ed) the true-

pioneers soil-
origined to

an instinct
ual-persist

ent creativ
ity.

a) My father

so childful
dream-eyed

(and yet) in
sistently

question
ing-down to

the root-
source.

b) Inspirat

ion (as-they-
used-to-call-

it) river
ed with an

archaical
ly-tidal

source-sense.

Nathaniel Pink (9)

a) planned so-

far-in-advan

ce that those
moments-of-

now seemed
less real than

the sky's time-
escaping

voice.

b) Multi-color

ed balloons
may have stimu

lated the
time-holding

depth of Pink'
s irresist

ible imaginat
ions.

c) Pink (an hab

itual man of
debonaire

self-certain
ed demeanor)

felt so pro
perly-suited

to the chall
enge of-each-

daily-task
that he often

forgot to
buttom-him

self up to
the truly in

habiting
length of his

(usually) un
matched self-

exposing col
ors.

d) Always a self-

confirming op
timist Pink

treaded the
down-to-earth

almost angeli
cally self-sus

pending.

e) Almost matt

er-of-factly
Pink took-to-

heart (though
rarely to his

tabled fare)
his mother'

s so warmly-
espousing

health-inclin
ation

s.

f) Pink

(though care
fully arm

ed against
the sweetness

of woman's
so subtle in

ducing tempt
ations)

suddenly
fell (almost

unawared) down
that slippery

well of irre
trievably

labyrinth
ed no-ways-

out.

g) They pre-mark

ed Nathaniel
Pink's size

able (and ad
equately com

fortable) grave-
stone(d)-habi

tation in his
most self-im

posing Capital-
Letters.

h) Pink oft

en listen
ed intense

ly self-con
firming to

the annuncia
ting sighs

of his own
audition

ed grave-
stone(d) ora

tions.

i) p. s.

(if one

might add a
shortened

addition to
Pink's multi

various life-
endeavor

s) He-took-it
all-in with

his usual self-
appreciating

modestly low-
toned appear

ances.

Spring

blossomed
into a pro

fusely color
ed landscape-

promising
with but

short-lived
expectat

ions.

Humor (3)

a) Is humor

(more or less
accessible

for some)
origined in an

oft pre-ordain
ed national-

concensus Or
can it become

intuned to
those still un

spoken moment'
s newly self-

effacing.

b) Frogged

I could still

become aroused
with Mark Twain'

s county-jump
ing prize-speci

man if old-
age hadn't

settled-me-down
to the phased-

length of such
smiling self-a

bandonment
s.

c) Jewish-humor

hits close-to-
the-mark of

protective
ly-affirming

self-inundat
ions.

Poemed (15)

a) Explain

ing poem
s is like

breaking
those secret

ly-espoused
rules of no-

wheres-but-
now.

b) Writing out-

of-the-dark
as stars be

coming invis
ibly-aware.

c) Attuned to

what will al
ways remain

incomplete
ly realiz

ed.

d) Moment

s of there
and alway

s-now.

e) Person

s and place
s (until

then) less
than self-i

magined.

f) As if color

s had become
interchange

ably other
wise.

g) No need of

more than
those inter

ior silence
s.

h) Beggar

s need to

continual
ly taste

what's be
come so whole

somely satis
fying.

i) Mountain

s erupt with
the incandes

cent glow of
a self-in

habiting
strangeness.

j) What we've

voiced was
always-known

but only-
now.

k) The beauty

of a woman
nakedly un

dressed for
your alway

s-intensing-
desire

s.

l) Squirrel

s air-borne
(though un

rehearsed)
pre-branch

ed for
their safe

ly-securing
landing-

right
s.

m) Why have

the winds so
suddenly

changed their
most intell

ing sense-of-
direction

s.

n) "the sun

also rise
s" its re

creating
light-invocat

ions.

o) Some exotic

birds caged
in the seldom

beauty of
their unknown

coloring
s.

3 Poems on Paintings of Wang Mian 14th C. (for Neil) (3)

a) Country Homes by Zhuchu

so densely
self-conceal

ing as if
swallowed-up

by nature'
s overswell.

*b) Plume Blossoms
Branches (1355)*

the fine
ness of ex

quisitely-
sensed trans

parancie
s.

*c) Straw-covered
Houses on Mt. Tai*

as if heaven
ly lifted bey

ond their spac
ious apparen

cies.

Indecision'

s like being
tentative

ly balanced
on both side

s to the
same quest

ion.

a) Seesaw

up in the
sun down in

the rain as
if weather

ed beyond
one's own

sense of
there-being.

b) Macke'

s hat-ladies
reflecting-

at-length
how it may

(or may not)
fit.

c) It seemed

(momentar

ily) as if
it could-have-

been just-the-
right-word.

d) The usually-

worn path two-
direction

ed in the
midst of an

equally-depth
ed wood.

e) He advised

(as if contem
plating aloud)

never marry un
less absolute

ly self-cer
tained.

f) That time-ap

pearing bird
not quite ade

quately branch
ed to but

an inquiet
ing inter

lude.

g) "To be or

not to be"
that Hamlet

ian dilemma
that can mark-

off each-of-
us at a most

unassuming-
moment.

He could al

most feel those
first-spring-

leaves ripen
into his

own fully-form
ed poetic-sens

sibilitie
s.

The distant

or the in-
the-midst-of

a wooded land
scape time-es

caping its
complete self-

encompass

ing.

a) The slowly

time-fading
loss of her

alcoholic-
husband

emptied-her-
down to those

dry-spells
of an Italian

ite summer.

b) She needed

to give her
all-encompass

ing the empti
ness of

what he'd
left of her

souled-down
person.

c) Those total

ly-engaged
often expect

(perhaps un
justly)

that other
s should re

spond in a
like-wise

manner.

Wearing my

father's used-
clothes should

have made-me-
feel into

his sense-of-
things a

thread-bare
imitation

of his ever-
changing mode

s-of-express
ion.

"Two roads ..." (9)

a) Some route

s become so
familiar

as repet
itive theme

s that alway
s lead (however

circuitious
ly involved)

to much the
same dead-

endings.

b) If we don'

t learn from
each and e

very indeci
pherable sign-

post then
life may teach

us its own
treacher

ously self-in
volving way

s.

c) She was

that self-re
liant-type

who could
only learn

life's old-
familiar-

lessons the
very-hardest-

of-ways.

d) Judas

I know You
have the power

to free-us
from the Roman-

bondage – my
will be done –

the real cause
of his cheap

sell-out from
the curse-in

voking cross-
ways of his

lord-and-
master.

e) Free-will

s its own
pre-deter

mining
end.

f) The low-

road of our
own self-e

vincing end
s and mean

s the high-
one of God'

s self-encom
passing judg

ment.

g) That St. Peter'

s rooster
crowed not at

its usual-
time but at

the dawn of
Peter's most

self-reveal
ing truth.

h) Could the

Judas-in-us
have betrayed

Christ for
fear-of-loss

of our own
self-sovereign

ty.

i) True faith

reveals its
own hidden-i

dentity only
when "Thy will

be done" pre-
determine

s our own
self-willing

life's-course.

Poetry books by David Jaffin

1. **Conformed to Stone,** Abelard-Schuman, New York 1968, London 1970.

2. **Emptied Spaces,** with an illustration by Jacques Lipschitz, Abelard-Schuman, London 1972.

3. **In the Glass of Winter,** Abelard-Schuman, London 1975, with an illustration by Mordechai Ardon.

4. **As One,** The Elizabeth Press, New Rochelle, N. Y. 1975.

5. **The Half of a Circle,** The Elizabeth Press, New Rochelle, N. Y. 1977.

6. **Space of,** The Elizabeth Press, New Rochelle, N. Y. 1978.

7. **Preceptions,** The Elizabeth Press, New Rochelle, N. Y. 1979.

8. **For the Finger's Want of Sound,** Shearsman Plymouth, England 1982.

9. **The Density for Color,** Shearsman Plymouth, England 1982.

10. **Selected Poems** with an illustration by Mordechai Ardon, English/Hebrew, Massada Publishers, Givatyim, Israel 1982.

11. **The Telling of Time,** Shearsman Books, Kentisbeare, England 2000 and Johannis, Lahr, Germany.

12. **That Sense for Meaning,** Shearsman Books, Kentisbeare, England 2001 and Johannis, Lahr, Germany.

13. **Into the timeless Deep,** Shearsman Books, Kentisbeare, England 2003 and Johannis, Lahr, Germany.

14. **A Birth in Seeing,** Shearsman Books, Exeter, England 2003 and Johannis, Lahr, Germany.

15. **Through Lost Silences,** Shearsman Books, Exeter, England 2003 and Johannis, Lahr, Germany.

16. **A voiced Awakening,** Shearsman Books, Exter, England 2004 and Johannis, Lahr, Germany.

17. **These Time-Shifting Thoughts**, Shearsman Books, Exeter, England 2005 and Johannis, Lahr, Germany.

18. **Intimacies of Sound,** Shearsman Books, Exeter, England 2005 and Johannis, Lahr, Germany.

19. **Dream Flow** with an illustration by Charles Seliger, Shearsman Books, Exeter, England 2006 and Johannis, Lahr, Germany.

20. **Sunstreams** with an illustration by Charles Seliger, Shearsman Books, Exeter, England 2007 and Johannis, Lahr, Germany.

21. **Thought Colors,** with an illustration by Charles Seliger, Shearsman Books, Exeter, England 2008 and Johannis, Lahr, Germany.

22. **Eye-Sensing,** Ahadada, Tokyo, Japan and Toronto, Canada 2008.

23. **Wind-phrasings,** with an illustration by Charles Seliger, Shearsman Books, Exeter, England 2009 and Johannis, Lahr, Germany.

24. **Time shadows,** with an illustration by Charles Seliger, Shearsman Books, Exeter, England 2009 and Johannis, Lahr, Germany.

25. **A World mapped-out,** with an illustration by Charles Seliger, Shearsman Books, Exeter, England 2010.

26. **Light Paths,** with an illustration by Charles Seliger, Shearsman Books, Exeter, England 2011 and Edition Wortschatz, Schwarzenfeld, Germany.

27. **Always Now,** with an illustration by Charles Seliger, Shearsman Books, Bristol, England 2012 and Edition Wortschatz, Schwarzenfeld, Germany.

28. **Labyrinthed,** with an illustration by Charles Seliger, Shearsman Books, Bristol, England 2012 and Edition Wortschatz, Schwarzenfeld, Germany.

29. **The Other Side of Self,** with an illustration by Charles Seliger, Shearsman Books, Bristol, England 2012 and Edition Wortschatz, Schwarzenfeld, Germany.

30. **Light Sources,** with an illustration by Charles Seliger, Shearsman Books, Bristol, England 2013 and Edition Wortschatz, Schwarzenfeld, Germany.

31. **Landing Rights,** with an illustration by Charles Seliger, Shearsman Books, Bristol, England 2014 and Edition Wortschatz, Schwarzenfeld, Germany.

32. **Listening to Silence,** with an illustration by Charles Seliger, Shearsman Books, Bristol, England 2014 and Edition Wortschatz, Schwarzenfeld, Germany.

33. **Taking Leave,** with an illustration by Mei Fêng, Shearsman Books, Bristol, England 2014 and Edition Wortschatz, Schwarzenfeld, Germany.

34. **Jewel Sensed,** with an illustration by Paul Klee, Shearsman Books, Bristol, England 2015 and Edition Wortschatz, Schwarzenfeld, Germany.

35. **Shadowing Images**, with an illustration by Pieter de Hooch, Shearsman Books, Bristol, England 2015 and Edition Wortschatz, Schwarzenfeld.

36. **Untouched Silences**, with an illustration by Paul Seehaus, Shearsman Books, Bristol, England 2016 and Edition Wortschatz, Schwarzenfeld.

Book on David Jaffin's poetry: Warren Fulton, **Poemed on a beach,** Ahadada, Tokyo, Japan and Toronto, Canada 2010.